MACHIAVELLI ON MODERN LEADERSHIP

MACHIAVELLI ON MODERN LEADERSHIP

WHY MACHIAVELLI'S IRON RULES ARE AS TIMELY AND IMPORTANT TODAY AS FIVE CENTURIES AGO

MICHAEL A. LEDEEN

TRUMAN TALLEY BOOKS
ST. MARTIN'S PRESS
NEW YORK

Frontispiece photo courtesy of Archive Photography,
a division of Archive Holdings, Inc.

MACHIAVELLI ON MODERN LEADERSHIP. Copyright © 1999 by
Michael A. Ledeen. All rights reserved. Printed in the United States
of America. No part of this book may be used or reproduced in any
manner whatsoever without written permission except in the case
of brief quotations embodied in critical articles or reviews. For information, address St. Martin's Press, 175 Fifth Avenue, New York,
N.Y. 10010.

Library of Congress Cataloging-in-Publication Data

Ledeen, Michael Arthur
    Machiavelli on modern leadership : why Machiavelli's iron
  rules are as timely and important today as five centuries ago /
  Michael A. Ledeen.—1st U.S. ed.
      p.   cm.
    Includes bibliographical references.
    ISBN 0-312-20471-X
    1. Machiavelli, Niccolò, 1469-1527—Contributions in political
  leadership.   2. Political leadership.   I. Title.
  JC143.M4L38   1999
  320.1'092—dc21   99-19366
                                                               CIP

First Edition: May 1999

10   9   8   7   6   5   4   3

CONTENTS

CONTENTS

WHY WORLD LEADERS
NEED MACHIAVELLI

The fighters in the elite Delta Force of the United States are as close to supermen as you are likely to find. Only the finest and toughest soldiers are invited to compete for a few hundred positions, and they undergo an intense physical and psychological ordeal to select the best of the best. Day after day they are made to march great distances with heavy backpacks, each man alone, with only a map and compass to find his way. They must maneuver through thick woods and across rivers and streams, for, while roads and trails are there, they are rarely the shortest route, and the men must cover the distance in a limited period of time. They are not told how quickly they must reach their destination, thus maximizing the stress. Food rations are given unevenly, abundant quantities one day, a meager supply the next. Those who have not conserved something from the day of plenty will be unable to perform satisfactorily on the lean day, which may last eighteen hours. They are required to be ready to go at a fixed time in the morning, but there is no alarm. Those who are not up, are out. They are under constant surveillance, but only rarely see the watchers, and they are never given any indication about the quality of their effort. The physical test is extreme, but it is the mental stress, compounded by isolation from one another, that breaks down all but the finest. Day by day, the number of survivors diminishes. It is rare that more than 25 percent of the candidates survive to the final phase.

By the end of the selection process—more than two and a half weeks—their body fat has been reduced to near zero, and they have been brought to the limit of psychological endurance. They are then ordered to undertake a final march over forty miles long, carrying a backpack weighing more than fifty pounds. Although, as usual, they do not know it, the time limit to complete the march is little more than a day. Sometime during the march, they begin to consume muscle, as there is no more fat to metabolize.

Physically spent and deprived of sleep for two full days, the handful of survivors are permitted to shower, and the very few who are officer candidates are then given a short book to read, along with a written examination. They are asked to relate the ideas presented in the book to their experiences during the selection process, and the missions they may be asked to lead if they are chosen to be officers of Delta Force. They have eighteen hours to convince their judges that they have understood the wisdom they have been ordered to read, and, although physically and psychologically exhausted, can apply it to tough, unpleasant tasks of the sort they may have to perform.

The book is *The Prince,* written in the early sixteenth century by Niccolò Machiavelli.

WHY MACHIAVELLI?

Nobody else has dealt with the political and moral requirements of leadership with such brutal clarity as Machiavelli. Machiavelli's thoughts about the proper use of power have always fascinated the greatest thinkers. My Italian edition of *The Prince* has a long introduction by Hegel, a great fan of Machiavelli; since the book's publication, virtually every major political philosopher has felt it necessary to write something on Machiavelli. Such obsessive attention bespeaks a passionate debate about Machiavelli's meaning and his standing. Forty years ago, Sir Isaiah Berlin counted twenty different interpretations, ranging from Machiavelli the Antichrist to Machiavelli the tortured humanist. This will surely surprise most of those who read *The Prince* in school, since few great books are as clearly and unambiguously written, but the debate continues. It would also surprise Machiavelli, because most of his work is intended for men and women of action, above all for leaders: leaders of religions, leaders of armies and of states, whether monarchical or republican, dictatorial or democratic. He spent most of his time in combat, on the battlefield or in the courtroom or the legislative chamber. He did not expect or desire to be carried off to scholarly libraries. He much preferred the company of military commanders, captains of industry, and men of state, and they have reciprocated his esteem. During the Italian campaign of the Second World War, the commanders of both armies—General Mark Clark of the United States and Field Marshal Albert Kesselring of Nazi Germany—declared Machiavelli's Tuscan estate in Sant'Andrea in Percussina off limits to their troops. Neither one wanted to be responsible for any damage to the historic site.

Machiavelli had plenty of opportunity to work with such leaders in the course of his career. His father was a modestly successful lawyer who mostly tended to his land and crops. The Machiavelli family's comfortable country villa—complete with Niccolò's desk and writing quill, where he used them— still stands in the minuscule village of Sant'Andrea in Percussina in the hills along the Florence–Siena road, and fine Chianti wine still comes from the Machiavelli vineyards and those of his neighbors. But Niccolò was also a city boy, an eager participant in the great artistic, musical, philosophical, and scientific explosion that was the Florentine Renaissance. His intellectual powers and seemingly inexhaustible energy—he fathered seven children, the last of which was born just two years before his death, at age fifty-seven—were recognized by the leaders of the Republic of Florence, and in the last years of the fifteenth century he was named secretary of the republic. It was a great job, a cross between today's White House chief of staff and ambassador-at-large, with additional military responsibilities thrown in for good measure. Until the downfall of the republic in 1512, Machiavelli not only participated in high-level policy discussions but also traveled throughout Europe, carrying messages to popes and kings, negotiating treaties and other agreements, organizing and training the militia, and commanding them in battle. He was a true workaholic and flourished under this high-tempo regime. But he did not sacrifice his heart and soul to his work; he found time for fun and for love, and, from his first days on the job, he wrote prolifically.

Anyone in Machiavelli's position would have to write a lot: his superiors expected full accounts of his travels, suggestions for legislation, reports on events of possible significance to the republic, and the like. Machiavelli, however, went far beyond these bureaucratic requirements, constantly searching for more general principles based on his experiences. Many of the famous rules for leaders in his books like *The Prince* and the *Discourses* were developed in hundreds of letters to friends and colleagues. A recent edition of Machiavelli's correspondence runs to 429 printed pages of rather small type, and this is only a portion of the entirety; over the centuries many letters have been lost.

Most of Machiavelli's literary creations were composed after his tenure as Florentine secretary, although even on the job he somehow found time to write several essays and a poetic chronicle about the major events of the times. From the very beginning the quality of his writing was very high, indeed, good enough to be plagiarized (after a successful lawsuit against the literary thief, the *First Decennial* was published under Machiavelli's own name). The major works, including successful dramas, histories, and books on politics and war, followed the downfall of the republic and the seizure of power by the Medici family in the autumn of 1512. Machiavelli was purged, banned from political activity, and sentenced to a year of internal exile within the boundaries of Florence. A few weeks later he was accused of plotting the overthrow of the Medici regime. He was thrown into prison, tortured over the course of a month, and ultimately found innocent. Banned from direct participation in politics, he followed the well-known dictum: those who can, do; those who can't, teach. Since he is forbidden to play the game, he'll coach, and, as publishing has just become relatively common, he can reach many of the players by writing books, and many more by staging plays.

He sets about his new career with the same passion and energy that carried him to the highest levels of the government of Florence.

When evening comes, I return home and enter my study; on the threshold I take off my workday clothes . . . and put on the garments of court and palace. Fitted out appropriately, I step inside the venerable courts of the ancients, where, solicitously received by them, I nourish myself on that food that *alone* is mine and for which I was born; where I am unashamed to converse with them and to question them about the motives for their actions, and they, out of their human kindness, answer me. And for four hours at a time I feel no boredom, I forget all my troubles, I do not dread poverty, and I am not terrified by death. . . . I have jotted down what I have profited from in their conversation and composed a short study.[1]

These famous lines from a letter to a close friend herald the appearance of *The Prince.* As he tells his friend, Machiavelli's examples are drawn from the past, above all from classical antiquity, which was appropriate to his Renaissance audience. Since our educational system no longer provides us with the knowledge necessary to appreciate or evaluate his examples, I have substituted many modern ones in the pages that follow. And since the rules are the same for leaders in all walks of life, I have included businessmen and sports figures along with military, political, and religious leaders. Instead of Borgias and Sforzas, Caesars and Medicis, you will find Ronald Reagan and Mikhail Gorbachev, Bill Gates and Warren Buffett, Leo Durocher and Vince Lombardi.

Machiavelli would welcome this update, although he would insist that anyone who wants to understand the dynamics of power and the methods of successful leadership must study history. It is not good enough to read the newspapers, or watch television, and try to understand today all by itself. Human nature doesn't change, above all at the top, where questions of success and survival are paramount and there is little time for the niceties. The serious study of the past provides the raw material for wise decisions today and tomorrow. We are prone to make the same kinds of mistakes our predecessors made, and we must emulate the great acts of past heroes.

Our own leaders badly need a refresher course. Among other blunders, they invariably give the wrong answer to one of Machiavelli's basic questions: Is it better to be more loved than feared, or more feared than loved? Western leaders from John Major and Bill Clinton to Newt Gingrich, Silvio Berlusconi, and Benjamin Netanyahu have desperately sought love from both friends and foes, to the ruin of their domestic and international enterprises. Ronald Reagan, Margaret Thatcher, Lee Kwan Yu, Bill Gates, and Pope John Paul II knew better, and reshaped the world.

One last question must be answered before plunging into the fray: How is it that after nearly five hundred years, Machiavelli's insights still challenge and inspire us so powerfully? Of course, he's a genius, "an Italian genius," as the philosopher Benedetto Croce rightly insisted, with the unique combination of wit, rhetorical flair, and ruthless analysis that characterizes the highest accomplishments of Italian thinkers. But there is more. In Renaissance Florence all received wisdom was being challenged by some of the greatest intellects, adventurers, and artists in history. New worlds were being discovered, new masterpieces created, and new ideas propounded with every passing month. Tumult and chaotic change were commonplace. The year after Machiavelli began working for the Florentine republic, 1498, Michelangelo finished the *Pietà*. The *David* was started shortly afterward; following its completion in 1504 it was placed in front of the Palazzo della Signoria, where Machiavelli's office was located. In 1505 Amerigo Vespucci set sail on his second voyage to the West Indies. Columbus's four voyages were complete, the Jews had been expelled from Spain the year of his first voyage—the same year that Lorenzo the Magnificent died (1492), and Portuguese explorers were laying claim to areas of the globe hitherto only guessed at. In 1510, when Machiavelli was a successful official in the Florentine government, Martin Luther went to Rome to lodge a protest against the corruption of the Catholic church. Nothing, it seemed, was being left unchallenged.

Machiavelli was part of this intellectual ferment, and thus both witnessed and participated in the birth pangs of the modern world. Being present at the creation, he was able to see with unusual clarity the fundamental rules of modern leadership, and he laid them down with brutal candor. As his Pulitzer Prize–winning biographer, Sebastian de Grazia, puts it: "Niccolò invents a new moral reasoning, and, more, redimensions the world, visible and invisible, balancing heaven and hell and making room for a different earth."[2] We inhabit that "different earth," and Machiavelli's rules are as valid for us as they were for the leaders he counseled five hundred years ago.

Prior to the Renaissance, the lord of a domain could protect himself against his foreign enemies by building a castle and a wall. If he were besieged, he could hire mercenaries or find allies to lift the siege; in the meantime his walls would protect him and his subjects. But by the time Machiavelli rose to a position of great power in the government of Florence, armies had artillery able to blow holes in the walls in minutes, and it would be too late to find allies or hired guns to defend the lord and his subjects as the enemy poured in through the breach. Now, survival would hinge on the willingness of the lord's people to fight and die for him. Convincing people to do this is a political task. It requires methods of leadership unknown or, as Machiavelli would say, forgotten in the Middle Ages. That is why Machiavelli insists on national armies, not mercenaries. He understands that soldiers in such armies need to be motivated. Dying for one's country does not come naturally; it requires belief in the worthiness of one's cause and the nobility of one's leaders. Modern politics are born from this necessity, and we moderns ignore it at our peril. Enemies are always ready to march, or fly, or launch.

Machiavelli rejects the simplistic notion that war is a drastic departure from normal behavior. Having studied history, Machiavelli knows that peace is rarer than war. We may not know who our next enemy will be, but we can be sure there will be one, and leaders who fail to prepare for the next war— on the battlefield, at the ballot box, or in the marketplace—are likely to be defeated. Machiavelli tells us how to design and implement winning strategies.

In addition to change, Machiavelli understands the role of luck. At the height of his powers, through no fault of his own, he is fired, imprisoned, tortured, and barred from the activities to which he has devoted nearly all his thoughts and passions. Bad luck! Licking his wounds, and turning his genius to writing, he spends the bulk of his time in a local inn, drinking, cursing, and playing backgammon and a Tuscan card game. Such games involve both luck and skill, and on any given occasion even the greatest player may be overwhelmed by a run of bad luck, even though, over time, the great player will win and the novice or duffer will be a loser. I suspect that Machiavelli's love of card games is of some importance in the development of his politics, for cardplayers live in a world quite different from that of players of board games. The board conceals nothing, and it is unnecessary to communicate with other players. In card games, most of the cards are concealed for much of each deal, and communication—whether through bidding or betting—is an integral part of the contest. Where there is communication, a whole new set of problems arises: if you tell all to your partner, your enemies obtain the same information, and it may be more valuable to them than to your ally. You may prefer to deceive them, but in so doing you risk inducing your partner to err before they do, thereby spelling ruin for your side.

It is no accident that this lover of card games appreciates the importance, and risk, of communication, including secrecy and deception. Machiavelli uses codes in some of his official correspondence and is one of the first political thinkers to exploit the new technology of printing to spread his ideas. He would be right at home in the upper levels of

Western corporations, where modern princes like Warren Buffett and Bill Gates spend many happy hours playing bridge, the game that best combines all these elements of communication with enormous technical challenges, yet preserves the element of luck that can wreck even the most brilliant plan or make a fool into the hero of the day.

Finally, like us Machiavelli is saddened, frustrated, sometimes even enraged by the sight of mediocre leadership, more corrupt than courageous, more self-indulgent than great of spirit. He knows from his study of history that men and women are often like that, but he also knows what greatness is and how it can be achieved by the best of us. He is not optimistic about the course of human affairs, but he does not shirk the challenge to engage it, and to educate and perhaps inspire a new breed of leader. He calls for those who care about their nation to risk everything, even their immortal souls, to achieve power and lift their people out of the moral slime into which they have fallen.

The purpose of *Machiavelli on Modern Leadership* is the same as his own: to present the basic principles of the proper and successful use of power in language that contemporary leaders can understand, the better to advance the common good. Like Machiavelli, we live at a moment of profound change in all areas of human endeavor. Just as he did, we see corruption reaching deep into Western societies at the very

moment we have soundly defeated many of our most dangerous enemies. Success, it turns out, carries its own risks, and
being top dog makes us more vulnerable to self-indulgence
and less attentive to the requirements of virtue that underlie
any enduring enterprise.

Machiavelli is commonly thought of as the ultimate cynic,
as an apologist for dictators. The adjective "Machiavellian"
has been hung on cruel leaders prepared to do anything to retain or increase their wealth and power. It may therefore be
surprising to discover that Machiavelli prefers free institutions to authoritarian ones, and reserves his greatest scorn for
tyrants. Machiavelli also has a great deal to say about the importance of religious faith and of virtue. He believes that,
along with good soldiers and good laws, the best state—the
one that rests upon the free activity of its citizens—requires
good religion. He considers Moses to be the greatest leader
because he created a new religion and a new state, and conversed with God. He believes fear of God underlies respect for
men. To be sure, his concept of Christianity is much at odds
with the prevailing theology and practice of his day. He considers the Roman Catholic church too corrupt and too soft. He
wants a tougher, more virile version of the faith, which will
inspire men to fight for the glory of their country, and he
wants a more spartan church, devoted to the glory of the spirit
rather than the tangible wealth of the papal court.

Ever the realist, he knows that leaders will sometimes have to violate religious strictures to prevail against merciless enemies and competitors, or to restore a corrupt enterprise to good health. But he condemns leaders who make cynical opportunism a trademark of their careers. He wants his leaders to be virtuous and to transmit virtuous standards to their followers.

Machiavelli uses the word "virtue" in many different ways, sometimes to mean "power," on occasion even as a reference to the erect male organ. In his play *The Ass* he writes:

> Not in one place did my hand stay;
> But running over her limbs,
> the lost virtue came back firm.

But he also uses it in the traditional sense of valor, worth, merit, moral perfection. That is very different from current usage, and, as the philosopher Leo Strauss once remarked, it is mysterious that "a word that used to mean the manliness of man has come to mean the chastity of women." But that is a different problem, and does not occupy us here. Machiavelli is of the old school, and he counts virtue, in its traditional sense, an essential ingredient—indeed, the highest possible achievement—of good leadership. This is its meaning in the pages that follow.

Brooding over Italian leaders' lack of virtue, Machiavelli finds little to surprise him. The corruption and disintegration of great enterprises is neither new nor shocking, after all. It is our history and our destiny. Even the most glorious human achievements, the creations of the most virtuous leaders, were usually short-lived. They have all fallen, more often than not because of internal decay. Moses' Israel was destroyed, as was Cyrus's Persian Empire. Theseus, the third in Machiavelli's trilogy of most glorious leaders, set Athens on the path to civilization, but the Golden Age of Periclean Athens lasted less than a century.

Machiavelli understands the pathology of this oft-fatal disease of the body politic. He has identified and catalogued the microbes that infect leaders' minds and spirits, dragging us down to ruin. Anyone looking at the modern world through Machiavelli's eyes will see, as he saw in his own day, an epidemic of corruption, causing a perilous shortage of virtuous leaders and a growing threat to freedom. His diagnosis helps us better understand our own problems and the qualities required of leaders capable of restoring virtue and preserving free institutions. Although he is not optimistic about the final outcome, he has a cure.

But it is a painful therapy.

CHAPTER ONE

THE COURSE OF HUMAN EVENTS

Human affairs being in a state of perpetual movement,
either ascending or declining . . .

If you're going to lead, you've got to fight. Whether you're on
the way up, are striving to acquire greater power, or are at the
top, fighting to maintain and expand it, you're involved in
struggle. And since, as Machiavelli tells us, "Men are more
ready for evil than for good," leaders and would-be leaders are
bloody-minded.

The bloody-mindedness derives from ambition, and human
ambition is unlimited, that of both individuals and the institutions they create. The struggle for power begins with the attempt to carve out a zone of freedom from others and
continues with the extension of domination over others. "First
[men] seek to secure themselves against attack; then they attack others."[1] First comes the fight for survival, or for freedom
from domination, then comes the "fight for ambition, which is

1

so powerful in human breasts that no matter to what rank they rise it never abandons them."[2] We have seen this process in many of the new democracies after the fall of the Soviet Empire. Heroic anti-Communists like Lech Walesa rather quickly developed a passion for power and continued to fight, no longer for a cause, but for their personal advancement. After defeating the Czech Communist dictatorship, Vaclav Havel became an international hero in part because he was a playwright who vowed to return to his literary endeavors after a brief period in government—but he is still in the Prague Castle.

The goal is power, which means the domination of others, and the winners revel in it, savoring what Machiavelli calls "the sweetness of domination." Power over others is an addictive drug that stimulates the desire for more of it. But that desire can never be fully satisfied; therefore, men, even the most powerful, are always unsatisfied. They want it all, but they can't have it. Since the desire for more power and wealth—the trappings of power—is always greater than our ability to accumulate them, he bluntly observes, "There continuously results from it a malcontentedness." Machiavelli does not believe that the haves are intrinsically different from the have-nots, nor innately superior. To be sure, they act differently, but that is simply the result of circumstance; men are "insolent when their affairs are prospering, and abjectly servile when adversity hits them." He knows that, given the chance, the have-nots will behave just as badly as the haves; it's all a question of opportunity, luck, and the grit, energy, determination, cunning, and tenacity—and sometimes wisdom—of those who maneuver for greater wealth and power.

The drive to expand is therefore built into all human institutions. Power and wealth are there for the having, and if you don't get them, somebody else will. It's an illusion, a potentially fatal illusion, to believe that your family, your country, your business, or your team, once comfortably and successfully established, can live happily ever after. You cannot opt out of this game. "It is impossible for a republic [or, in fact, any other human institution] to remain long in the quiet enjoyment of her freedom within her limited confines," Machiavelli lectures us,

> For even if she does not molest others, others will molest her, and from being thus molested will spring the desire and the necessity of conquests, and even if she has no foreign foes, she will find domestic enemies amongst her own citizens.[3]

TURMOIL

Change—above all, violent change—is the essence of human history. Machiavelli tells a story of the origins of political systems that is all about constant turmoil.[4] Early on, when there were few people, we didn't need governments, because mankind was scattered in small bands. But after a while larger groups formed, and each chose the strongest, bravest man as its leader. In that condition of rudimentary government—a primitive form of enlightened despotism, or the Good Czar—men learned to distinguish "what is honest and good from what is pernicious and wicked." He's not talking about ultimate values, but about politics, about the relationship between ruler and subjects:

> The sight of someone injuring his benefactor evoked in them hatred and sympathy and they blamed the ungrateful and respected those who showed gratitude, well aware that the same injuries might have been done to themselves. Hence to prevent evil of this kind they took to making laws and to assigning punishments to those who contravened them. The notion of justice thus came into being.

Once the laws were in place, we no longer needed a warrior in charge; indeed, it was better to have a more prudent leader, one primarily concerned with preserving justice. That was the first Good State, its goodness guaranteed by laws rather than by the qualities of a single leader. But it didn't last. After a while, leadership became hereditary, and subsequent leaders sank into degeneracy, devoting themselves to excesses of "extravagance, lasciviousness, and every other form of licentiousness." The people hated the corrupt new leaders, and the leaders, fearful of the righteous indignation of the people, created a tyranny. This was a Bad State, and thankfully it did not last either.

Good men, "conspicuous for their liberality, magnanimity, wealth, and ability," organized conspiracies against the tyrant and rallied the people. Once the tyrant was overthrown, the leaders of the revolution were determined to avoid the concentration of power in the hands of a single leader, and so organized a virtuous aristocracy that took care to reassert the primacy of the old, good laws. The aristocrats "subordinated their own convenience to the common advantage and, both in private matters and public affairs, governed and preserved order with the utmost diligence." Another Good State—it, too, destined to fall in short order.

New aristocrats then came to power who "had no experience of the changeability of fortune," and took their power for granted, assuming it would last forever. They sank into degeneracy, just like the descendants of the Good Czar. Power became hereditary, greed and licentiousness became widespread, civic rights were disregarded, and an evil oligarchy took over. In time, the people came to hate the oligarchs, and, inspired by a suitable leader, destroyed them. And since they had by now learned that the Good Czar became a tyrant, and the noble aristocrats became corrupt oligarchs, the people created a democracy, with safeguards against the accumulation of power by either a strong individual or a limited group. This was the third form of good government, and it, too, was short-lived. Within a generation, democracy degenerated into anarchy, and a new strong leader emerged to restore order, thus starting the cycle all over again.

If there were no foreign enemies, the cycle might go on forever, but in practice, very few states survive long enough to return to Go. During one of its moments of degeneracy, weakness, or chaos, a stronger neighbor takes it over or wipes it out.

It's a political fairy tale, and like all good fairy tales it tells us some basic things about ourselves. Machiavelli reminds us that all political systems are fragile and can be toppled from either within or without. Given the history of the race, it should surprise no one when rulers fall, or when one country is conquered by another, or even when mass uprisings take place. Such events are in the nature of politics, because each type of government is fundamentally defective. The good ones—the Good Czar, the noble aristocracy, and the pure democracy—tend to be short-lived, while the bad ones—the Bad Czar and the oligarchy—are hateful and vicious, provoking violent opposition that eventually leads to their ruin. Anarchy simply opens the door to a new tyranny.

As nations and empires come and go, so do the other ambitious human enterprises. Eastern Airlines is gone, along with Pan Am, once the greatest airline in the world. Packard automobiles are gone, along with the gorgeous Bugattis, Studebakers, and Dusenbergs. Fokker is gone, along with Curtis Wright, Douglas, Grumman, McDonnell, Sud Aviation, Vickers, and De Havilland, all glorious successes in bygone days of aviation, all either vanished entirely or gobbled up by their enemies. Great banks like BCCI, First American, and Banco Ambrosiano are gone, too, and Woolworth stores, archetypes of our national life, have closed all over America. Royal families are gone to their graves, like the Romanovs, or into exile, like the Italian House of Savoy and its counterparts from Greece, Libya, Bulgaria, Albania, Iran, and Romania. George Bush, at one time the most popular president in the history of the United States, was defeated a few months later by Bill Clinton, an obscure governor of the inconsequential state of Arkansas.

The tempo may vary from moment to moment, but stability exists only in the grave, not in this life. It therefore behooves the man or woman of action (Machiavelli is well aware of the greatness of women), and especially those who would lead great enterprises, to be ready at all times to change strategies and tactics. As Emerson said, "A foolish consistency is the hobgoblin of little minds, adored by little statesmen and philosophers and divines. With consistency a great soul has simply nothing to do."[5]

On the eve of the Battle of Waterloo, in 1815, the Duke of Wellington was asked by one of his generals to describe his strategy for the next day, so that in the event Wellington fell, the others would be able to carry out his master plan to defeat Napoleon's armies. Wellington was flabbergasted by the question. "If you want to know my plan," he replied, "you must first tell me what Bonaparte is going to do." Wellington intended to win by watching what his enemies did, and then acting accordingly, a flexible strategy entirely in keeping with Machiavelli's view of the world. Successful leaders have to be ready to change their methods, because conditions are very difficult to predict in the first place, and even if you get it right at the beginning, things are going to keep on changing.

"Anyone wise enough to understand the times and types of affairs," Machiavelli tells us in one of his typical "good news/bad news" phrases, "would always have good fortune . . . [and] the wise man would rule the stars and the Fates." He doesn't entirely believe this—as we'll see, he is in great awe of Fortune—and he knows that no one is wise enough to understand the times for very long. The imperative for leaders is absolute: get ready to change.

THE CHANGE ARTISTS

On Wall Street or Main Street, as in politics, athletics, or war, success most often goes to the person who sees that he has made a mistake and quickly changes, or to someone who senses that a winning strategy is running out of time, and abandons it, even while others are copying him. Winning leaders are invariably good "game coaches," because they are the first to see how things are going, they quickly figure out why, and then they make the appropriate changes. How many times have you seen a football or basketball game turn around dramatically at halftime? The "halftime adjustments" are just like Wellington's improvisations on the battlefield, once he came under Napoleon's attack.

Some coaches have been able to change their methods in accordance with the players under their guidance. For example, the basketball coach Pat Riley has produced winning teams with radically different styles, each suited to the talent on the team. His championship teams in Los Angeles featured razzle-dazzle ball handling and fast breaks. In New York, the Knicks were a slow, deliberate team whose personality rested on tough defense. Then, in Miami, Riley showed he could win even with mediocre talent that had been decimated by injury and demoralized by the loss of two star players. Using different methods in different circumstances, adapting himself to the changing challenges he found, Riley repeatedly adjusted his way of doing things to the conditions of his times. It's a rare enough phenomenon, but even rarer is the leader who can change careers without a drop in brilliance. We can count them on our fingers.

George Washington was first a political figure, then a military leader, then a great president. Charles de Gaulle and Dwight Eisenhower, distinguished military leaders, became outstanding presidents. Napoleon was a military genius whose contributions to politics and the rule of law—the Napoleonic Code—will long outlast the effects of his military prowess. Colin Powell was a successful military leader who has become a political figure and would like to become president. There aren't many like them. The success of these select few shows how rare are those who excel in more than one kind of endeavor—individuals known as Renaissance men.

Of the current generation of global business leaders, no one embodies the flexibility Machiavelli writes about as well as Bill Gates of Microsoft. Gates set out to become a lawyer but left Harvard in 1975, when a close friend who was a mathematical whiz, Paul Allen, convinced him that Intel's new 8080 microprocessor chip had made home computers possible. Unlike some of their early competitors, who hitched their wagons to specific products or concepts, Gates and Allen set out to please the customer—all the customers they could reach. At each stage of Microsoft's evolution, Gates was building on the work of other people, trying to adapt Microsoft's products to fit well with the latest hardware and the jazziest software. Gates and Allen created the programming language, Basic, for the first really popular microcomputer, the Altair. Basic was produced in as many versions as there were separate microprocessors and separate operating systems. Gates wanted his language in all computers, whatever they were like, and wherever they were operating. From the beginning, Microsoft products were sold in the United States, Europe, and Japan. This strategy required considerable flexibility, as Gates would have to be able to adjust to rapid changes in three very different markets with three very different cultures.

Gates is a great Machiavellian because he built change and flexibility into Microsoft from the very beginning and because, while he ruthlessly fought to dominate the market, he never tried to dominate its direction; he concentrated on understanding where it was headed and then becoming the dominant force in the next phase. Basic was the first example of Gates's strategy; two more followed: DOS/Windows and Internet Explorer. The success of Basic was the result of hard work and a sound fundamental insight into the emerging computer market.

For the most part, leaders do *not* change with the times, for two very good reasons. First, we can't change our own natures (so if we're poorly suited for the changed conditions, we're doomed). The second reason is, paradoxically, derived from the nature of successful people. Having succeeded in the past, they assume that the same methods that got them there will keep them on top. "It is this," Machiavelli reminds us, "that causes the varying success of a man; for the times change, but he does not." And not merely a man alone; "the ruin of states is caused in like manner."

There are even some areas of competitive activity, such as the real estate business, in which failure to change, and hence the ruin of the leader, seems almost an integral part of the thing. Real estate values fluctuate with inflation, and anyone who adopts Machiavelli's methods and studies the history of real estate investments quickly sees that periods of inflation are inevitably followed by deflations. Investors who fail to protect against future declines in value can be severely damaged. This has been said over and over again by both analysts and practitioners, yet real estate tycoons continue to fall prey to the should-have-been-expected deflationary swings. They are encouraged in their folly by the tax laws, which almost everywhere take a substantial bite out of capital gains. Not wanting to pay the taxes, the real estate magnates seek to recycle their profits. The typical real estate empire is therefore highly leveraged, as profits are constantly plowed back into new, bigger investments, thereby making it even more difficult to cash out in time.

The most recent example of this recurring catastrophe is the spectacular collapse of the Reichmann empire in the early

1990s. Immigrants to Canada in the mid-fifties, they started a tile importing business, did very well, and invested their profits in Toronto land. These investments did even better, and their firm, Olympia & York, expanded rapidly to become Canada's leading real estate company. By the late seventies they had become a force in the United States and England as well. Barely a decade later, Olympia & York was a vast real estate empire that had become the biggest landlords in Manhattan and embarked upon a multi-billion-dollar project in London known as Canary Wharf. This grandiose undertaking proved to be the Reichmann's undoing. To finance Canary Wharf they borrowed heavily against the paper value of their other holdings and the value of their reputation as infallible investors.

Had the cost of money remained relatively constant or, better yet, declined, the Reichmanns would have succeeded, but interest rates went up, driven by the unexpected fall of the Berlin Wall and the rapid reunification of Germany. The West Germans, forced to absorb the enormous costs associated with the integration of East Germany and obsessed as always with the fear of runaway inflation, raised interest rates on the deutschmark. Other currencies followed suit, and the Reichmanns suddenly found themselves unable to meet the payments on their huge loans. Olympia & York crashed. From being one of the greatest financial empires in the world, Olympia & York became one of the greatest business failures in history. The Reichmanns did not anticipate the change in circumstances and were unable to adapt fast enough when it occurred.

Even great leaders can easily fall victim to a dramatic change in circumstance. Winston Churchill was a demigod during the Second World War, but once the fascists were defeated he was voted out of office. George Bush was judged unsuited to handle the post–Gulf War issues facing America. In part such failures derive from the ingratitude of the people, a subject to which Machiavelli devotes a rhyme:

> So it happens that often one toils in serving,
> and then for good service brings back
> miserable life and violent death.
> Therefore, Ingratitude not being dead,
> everyone must flee the courts and states:
> for there is no shorter road to lead man
> to weep over what he wished for, once he got it.[6]

But most of the time the primary ingredient is the leader's inability to adapt to the turmoil of human events.

WAR, AND OTHER NORMAL THINGS

We twentieth-century people shouldn't need this reminder; after all, we've lived through the most revolutionary period in human history. This century began with the fall of the Austro-Hungarian and Ottoman empires and ended with the implosion of the Soviet Empire, and in between the end of colonialism and the defeat of the fascists thrown in for extras. In the past quarter century alone, so many tyrants have fallen all over the world that nobody can remember their names anymore (can *you* name the last Communist dictators of East Germany and Hungary?). The United States has won three world wars, culminating with the amazing, virtually bloodless victory over the Soviet Empire at the end of the Cold War. Nonetheless, the vast majority of Americans believe that peace is the normal condition of mankind, and are constantly astonished (and sometimes quite annoyed) at outbreaks of war or more limited forms of violence, such as insurrection, revolution, assassination, riots, and the like. You might have thought that this most bloody and turbulent century would have taught us that peace is not normal, and that it is best to prepare for the next war, to be sure of winning it at the least cost. No! Each time, the armed forces have been dramatically reduced, the "boys" have been "brought home," and the public has largely lost interest in foreign policy, believing that this time, at long last, a stable peace has finally been established. In this unfortunate manner, the seeds of the next catastrophe are sown before the defeated enemy's body grows cold.

Peace is *not* the normal condition of mankind. War and the

preparation for war are the themes of human history. Centuries like the nineteenth—when Europe experienced a rare interregnum of relative tranquillity between the end of the Napoleonic Wars and the outbreak of the First World War—are rare. Bloody conflicts are history's leitmotif. Any leader who believes otherwise will go to his ruin, or at least risk it.

Conflict is not the consequence of the rational pursuit of self-interest, either by states or by individuals; it flows straight from the deepest wellsprings of human nature. It is not an aberration, nor does it come from a failure of understanding; it is an integral, inescapable part of what we are. It applies to all human activities, foreign and domestic, scholarly and athletic, in enterprise as in the pursuits of people of faith. Woe betide us if we are unprepared for war, either on the battlefield itself or in other forms: domestic uprisings or terrorism, ruthless business or athletic competition. Our challengers, whether new teams in the league or Japanese companies making cheaper and better automobiles, will not be charmed by sweet reasonableness, for they seek domination over us. If you're going to be a leader, you must make a simple choice: either dominate or be dominated.

This being the case, all those noble efforts to prevent war by "educating" people to solve their problems peaceably or by drafting treaties making all war, or certain kinds of warfare, illegal not only are destined to fail but will actually make things even worse. As Donald Kagan tells us in his celebrated study *On the Origins of War and the Preservation of Peace,* "Good will, unilateral disarmament, the avoidance of alliances, teaching and preaching of the evils of war by those states who . . . seek to preserve peace, are of no avail."[7] Beware of those who, assuming that war is a thing of the past, tell us we must only prepare for peace. They are far more dangerous than those who, understanding human nature, prepare for war.

SUNDAY, JULY 6, 1997. PHILADELPHIA (Reuters)— Media mogul Ted Turner took the stage as an Independence Day statesman Friday and called for a national vote on replacing the "Star-Spangled Banner" with a less "warlike" anthem.

Turner, who received the annual Philadelphia Liberty Medal for his founding of CNN, urged that "America the Beautiful" be adopted as the U.S. national anthem now that much of the world was free of armed conflict.

"It should be changed because 'The Star-Spangled Banner' is a war song," Turner said in a medal ceremony. . . . "Now the whole western hemisphere is at peace, most of the world's at peace. It's time to change with the times because brotherhood is a lot more important than military force and that's what 'America the Beautiful' is all about," he said.

Ted Turner, of all people, should know better, for his life has been a constant battle as he has built victorious racing ships, exceptional professional athletic teams, and the world's most popular news network. Had anyone said to him, "Don't start CNN, the networks are at peace with one another," he'd have dismissed the remark as unworthy of a serious person. Nations are no less aggressive than entrepreneurs.

Those who pursue peace at all costs and do not take the necessary steps to defend themselves against the next attack risk something Machiavelli deems even more terrible than fighting: defeat and domination by their enemies. If you don't fight, you're going to be dominated by the winners. It's better to be a winner yourself, because you will then dominate, which—for a while, anyway—means you've got at least one less enemy to worry about. The military commentator Flavius Vegetius Renatus had it all figured out in the fourth century: "Let him who desires peace, prepare for war." Kagan echoes the thought:

> What works best, even though imperfectly, is the possession by those states who wish to preserve the peace of the preponderant power and of the will to accept the burdens and responsibilities required to achieve that purpose.[8]

That is why one of the leading Machiavellians of modern times, the Green Bay Packers legendary coach Vincent Lombardi, was right to say "Winning is not the most important thing; it's the only thing." If we are dominated, it's probably our own fault. William Shakespeare, who knew his Machiavelli well, put it in verse: "The fault, dear Brutus, is not in our stars / But in ourselves, that we are underlings." Those prepared to learn from Machiavelli never make this mistake. The young François Mitterrand, writing to his sister in 1938, the year Neville Chamberlain appeased Hitler and abandoned Czechoslovakia to the armies of the Third Reich, drafted his life's motto: "All leads to this: to win or to lose. As things never remain stationary, not moving means to begin to lose."[9]

Of course, nobody said it was going to be easy. "How hard it is to win!" Mitterrand lamented. "So much patient work is required! Nothing can be overlooked, no little action, no minuscule event." Not to worry; it's worth it. The winners get all the fun, and all the glory. Those who say the most important thing is how you play the game just don't understand, for you will be hailed no matter how you played . . . so long as you win. The replays may show that Michael Jordan often got preferential treatment from the referees, but that doesn't dim his glory or diminish the adulation of basketball fans. Jordan got special respect because he was a great leader. He earned his glory by his remarkable string of championships, unique in the history of basketball. Movie stars rarely lead exemplary lives, but their beauty and elegance—Machiavelli would call it grandeur—and their great wealth make them heroes.

These are mild examples of the overwhelming popularity

of the victors; the more important cases are political, of which the most dramatic are surely the greatest mass murderers of this century of mass murder, Hitler, Stalin, and Mao. Hitler was revered by his people, and there was no effective resistance to Nazism until the Germans were defeated on the battlefield. When Stalin died, millions of Russians—the overwhelming majority simple souls, not politically active or ambitious people—stood hour after hour in line to parade past the cadaver lying in state in the Kremlin. Rivers of tears were shed, and the chorus of sobs was incessant. Yet Stalin had ordered the murder of tens of millions of innocents. A similar scene followed the death of Mao, who caused even more to be murdered in the most ghastly ways, even including cannibalism, during the Cultural Revolution a mere thirty years ago.[10] It would be easy to write off these displays of emotion as spurious, the people fearing to be accused of insufficient adoration of the great leader. Yet we know from firsthand accounts, many of them from men and women who rebelled against the Communist tyrannies, that the grief was genuine, as was the reverence felt for the tyrants during their years of grandeur. One such anti-Communist, Alexander Zinoviev, writes that Stalin and the instruments of his terror—the so-called "organs of state security" such as the KGB—had the full support of most of the people, and not because they feared the terror (the "simple" people were rarely directly terrorized, and indeed found in the "organs" the only truly efficient institution in the system to which they could turn for help in solving the problems of their daily lives, such as household repairs). "On the contrary, the 'organs' were venerated as the instruments of supreme justice"—that is to say, of Stalin's will.[11]

You might suspect from all this that Machiavelli is like the big-screen version of General George Patton, someone who loves war, even finding it spiritually fulfilling. Not at all. He has created militias, gone to war, and organized both victorious and losing campaigns. Machiavelli is not an armchair general; he knows full well how terrible war is. But he also knows that there can be no satisfactory escape from the fight. John Keegan, the *London Telegraph*'s military correspondent, would agree.

When starting out in this genre, I believed that if the world could be informed of the truths of combat, future generations might be deterred from it. Experience has disabused me. Telling does not deter and knowing does not inoculate. War will always find men to fight it.[12]

"One does not remove war or escape from its terrible grasp," Machiavelli advises leaders-to-be. "One postpones it to the advantage of others." Since it's going to happen sooner or later, it's best to fight under the conditions most favorable to *you*. In the early eighties, Israel discovered that Iraq was developing nuclear weapons. Instead of postponing conflict with Iraq to a time when Saddam Hussein could attack Israel with atomic bombs, the Israelis struck first, and destroyed the Iraqi nuclear reactor at Osiris. Japan's attack on Pearl Harbor in 1941 was inspired by the same Machiavellian logic. Knowing they would have to fight America sooner or later, the Japanese chose to attack when they were strong, and we were weak. Our declarations of neutrality were not believed, and would not have helped us even if they had been.

If our leaders had paid more attention to Machiavelli, they might have avoided the Pearl Harbor disaster, for Machiavelli warns that if there's a war going on in your neighborhood, it is more dangerous to be neutral than to take sides. If you stay out, you'll be hated by the loser and despised by the winner. You will be considered "a useless ally and an undreaded enemy," and thus likely to be attacked in the future. The Japanese, driven by the urge to dominate, showed no mercy. Your enemies never do.

Machiavelli had abundant firsthand evidence from his childhood in Florence to support his conviction that good leaders must always be ready for the next attack. When he was just nine years old there was a failed coup attempt, aimed against the ruling family, the Medicis, by the other great merchant bankers of the period, the Pazzi. The plot was well conceived and had powerful backing from none other than the pope, and the archbishop of Florence was one of the principal conspirators. They planned to assassinate Lorenzo de' Medici—

the philosopher-prince who became known as Lorenzo "the Magnificent"—and his brother while they knelt in prayer in church, and then proclaim a new government, as troops loyal to the Pazzi closed in on the government buildings. Lorenzo's brother was killed, but Lorenzo himself survived the attack; thanks to a combination of his own courage and the toughness of the Florentine government officials, the people rallied to the Medici and turned on the Pazzi.

The vengeance that was delivered on the Pazzi was of biblical ferocity. The archbishop was seized and hung in his robes from a window high in the governmental palace (there is a sketch by Leonardo to document the details). Many Pazzi were killed in the streets, some literally torn limb from limb, and the unrestrained assault against the Pazzi and their allies continued for weeks. Others were captured and subjected to every imaginable form of torture, including being roasted, feet first, over an open fire. Each time one of the leaders was executed, Botticelli decorated the wall of the Bargello Palace with a small painting of the event, and Lorenzo would frequently add a caption in verse, describing the moral shortcomings of the unfortunate man and giving an account of his death. Even this was not enough to slake the thirst for revenge; the body of the ringleader was torn from his grave and burned to ash, and the ashes were scattered in the Arno River, so that the soil of the city would not be polluted by the flesh of the villain.

The Medici systematically eliminated all evidence of the existence of the Pazzi. Their names were erased from the facades of their palaces, references to them were expunged from lists of praiseworthy citizens past and present, paintings and frescoes with their images were destroyed or covered up. No wonder that the Tuscan word for "fools" is *pazzi!*

Had the Medici been better prepared, they would have struck first. But they were well prepared to fight once the Pazzi attacked, gave no quarter in the struggle, and achieved a glorious victory.

PREPARATION FOR COMBAT

So it is not just a matter of being prepared for change, as if change were something that somehow "just happens" (even though, when luck intervenes, it just does). Leaders must constantly be on a war footing, soldiers at the ready, weapons loaded. No accident, then, that successful business leaders are "captains of industry," or that sports are replete with military metaphor, from grand slams in baseball, bridge, and tennis to football's trenches and bombs, the omnipresent "sudden death" in soccer, hockey, and football, and basketball players called forwards and guards. All people involved in these highly competitive endeavors know they had better be ready to fight, because they're certainly going to be attacked. Any businessman or sports leader who permits himself to be surprised by his competition will soon be looking for another job, and the shareholders or fans will celebrate his departure. Paradoxically—Machiavelli often exposes paradoxes where we least expect them—it is political and military leaders who most often seem uncomfortable with their own armies and with the use of force in any but the most desperate circumstances.

In America, reluctance to use military force is typically linked to the "Vietnam syndrome," and indeed the rationale for only using military power in extremis was formulated by men who fought in the disastrous war in Southeast Asia. Having lost domestic political support and been forced to abandon the battlefield, and then having been derided and humiliated upon their return to America, the generation of military leaders who rose to the highest ranks of the armed forces in the late seventies and eighties determined never again to risk American lives in combat unless they were certain of a strong domestic consensus. This typically American notion was originally known as the "Weinberger doctrine"—Secretary of Defense Caspar Weinberger first presented it in a speech in November 1984—and its central theme was the following:

Before the U.S. commits combat forces abroad, there must be some reasonable assurance we will have the support of the American people and their elected representatives in Congress. We cannot fight a battle with the Congress at home while asking our troops to win a war overseas, or, as in the case of Vietnam, in effect asking our troops not to win but just to be there.[13]

This mischievous notion was subsequently embraced by General Colin Powell—who added the requirement of a clearly defined "exit strategy"—and was endorsed by virtually all prominent military and civilian leaders in the Bush and Clinton administrations.

Machiavelli rejects the presumption that original expectations will be fulfilled, because the first rule of human events is change. Things will *not* work out as you expect. Steve Jobs assumed that the Mac and the Lisa would have the same euphoric market reception as the Apple and refused to change his game plan, even when it should have been obvious that the world had changed. The defeat not only was devastating for his company's profits, but, as confidence in him was decisively undermined, it also savaged his own capacity to lead Apple back to the top of the PC world.

Weinberger and Powell knew that events on the battlefield would change, but they presumed that, once you've got consensus, you'll keep it for the whole mission, and everyone will cheer when you get back, so long as you haven't lost too many men and women. Machiavelli proclaimed such a notion to be nonsense, because consensus goes to the victor alone. The people will despise a defeated leader, no matter how great their initial enthusiasm. At the beginning of the movie *Patton,* the general pronounces the magic Machiavellian words "The American people hate a loser." If you win, you're a hero; if you lose, you're a bum. Consensus at the outset of the operation won't serve you any better today than it did in Vietnam, when initial public support for the war was solid; it remained strong until very late in the day. Public opinion turned against the war only when it became clear that we were not going to win.

The advocates of the Weinberger/Powell doctrines have tried to get around these objections by dumbing down the concept of victory, as seen in two go-rounds with the Iraqi dictator Saddam Hussein. The first was the Gulf War, which one wag has elegantly defined "victory interruptus."[14] The Bush administration, including Powell himself, suddenly and unexpectedly called off our armies just at the moment when Saddam's core force, the Republican Guard, was about to be destroyed, and with them, the regime itself. Not that we didn't want Saddam out of the way; Bush publicly murmured that it would be a fine thing if the Kurds and Shi'ites were to rise and rid the world of the butcher of Baghdad. But when they took the president seriously and started shooting, American military support was nowhere to be seen, and they were slaughtered. As a conscience-balm, we and some of our allies created a safe zone in the north of Iraq, where the Kurdish and Shi'ite refugees could survive, and we parachuted food and cold-weather gear to them as winter set in.

Ever since then, the Bush/Powell apologists have strived mightily to convince the world that we won a wonderful victory, that we were right to permit the Republican Guard to survive, and that it would actually have been a grave mistake for us to bring down Saddam's evil regime, because we would have become mired in a Vietnamlike swamp. But the crucial fact remains: Saddam survived with his military sufficiently intact to stay in power and massacre his enemies. A perilous lesson had been taught to all those who might contemplate challenging the United States: the Americans will not stay the course, they will not fight until true victory is achieved, they will not dominate you. Even if events on the battlefield are ruinous for you, you will live to fight another day.

When the next fighting day arrived for Saddam Hussein, Bill Clinton dumbed down victory even further. In the summer of 1996, Saddam challenged the safe haven in the north, sending hundreds of tanks against the Kurds and Shi'ites there after some of them had assembled resistance groups to challenge his rule. We were well aware of Saddam's preparations, and had promised the anti-Saddam forces—whom we had supported in a halfhearted way—that there would be a speedy and forceful response if the invasion came off.

We watched Saddam assemble his armored column, composed of virtually every operational tank in Iraq, more than three hundred in all. We watched him advance slowly northward, and we sent him warnings of dire consequences. We had plenty of time to send attacking planes from bases in Turkey or from carriers in the Persian Gulf. In open country, with no problems of weather or terrain, the Iraqi tanks would have been sitting ducks for our fighter-bombers. If we had attacked the Iraqi tank column, it would have been a real blow to Saddam, would have sent a much-needed morale boost to his opponents, and would have made it clear to everyone in the region that the United States was serious about defending our friends and advancing our interests. Instead, Bill Clinton told his foreign policy people that his top priority was to avoid American casualties of any sort: no body bags delivered to weeping families back home, no planes shot down over hostile territory, no hostages dragged behind jeeps through dusty streets. Therefore no risk, and therefore no serious action. The cruise missiles belatedly lobbed into radar and anti-aircraft bases in southern Iraq neatly demonstrated the president's obsession with keeping Americans out of harm's way, and its ruinous consequences: freedom fighters died instead of stormtroopers, Saddam was much stronger and we were much weaker than before the Iraqi blitz. In the end, the United States Air Force flew more than two thousand Kurdish and Iraqi chauffeurs, secretaries, janitors, bottle washers, and their dependents—all supporters of the anti-Saddam resistance—to safety on the island of Guam.

Nearly two years later, Saddam once again challenged the United States by expelling American inspectors from Iraq. Once again, Clinton dithered and delayed, sent troops to the Gulf region, threatened harsh action, but in the end did nothing except sign on to an ineffective agreement negotiated by United Nations Secretary General Kofi Annan, that gave Saddam time to relocate his weapons of mass destruction from the sites the Americans wanted to look at.

Finally, in December 1998, Clinton ordered three days of bombing, after Saddam reneged on the latest agreement. By then it was clear to most everyone that Clinton had no serious strategy to deal with Iraq.

In the *Discourses,* Machiavelli neatly characterizes this kind of behavior: "When these indolent princes or effeminate republics send a general with an army into the field, the wisest order they think they can give him is never to risk a battle, and above all things avoid a general action."[15]

We'll get back to "indolent" and "effeminate" shortly; the point here is that good leaders recognize that conflict is omnipresent, and they rightly prepare to fight and win. Leaders who tell their soldiers that the avoidance of injury is the most important thing are doomed. Nations that spurn victory in the name of safety end in death and defeat. Can you imagine Vince Lombardi sending his champion football team on the field with the injunction, "Don't get hurt"?

Worse still, when you find a leader who acts that way, you

can be sure that he's making other big mistakes as well, because the proper use of power is such a central ingredient in any good organization. Indeed, at one point Machiavelli goes so far as to argue that "the foundation of states is good military organization. . . . Without such a military organization, there can neither be good laws nor anything else good." He's not only talking about armies, but about all leaders, from corporate executives to the armed men and women who provide domestic security by defending institutions and leaders and arresting criminals. Our institutions are not only targets from without; we have to be ready to combat evil in our own midst just as vigorously as we fight foreign invaders. As Mitterrand lamented to his sister, there's an enormous amount of work to do.

Machiavelli is also talking about the selflessness required of all those who serve the common interest. He is alarmed whenever he sees leaders putting their personal desires before the goals of the institutions they command. A good soldier is willing to sacrifice his life for victory, and a good leader must be willing to sacrifice his own personal ambition for the success of the institution he commands. To achieve victory, the first step is to see the world plain, to accept the facts about human nature, and to act vigorously to dominate, lest we be dominated by others.

The second step is an act of humility: to recognize that there are forces we cannot always control. We may win without merit and lose without shame. Sometimes Fortune destroys the best-laid plans of even the greatest leaders.

CHAPTER TWO

LUCK

---

*And if anyone might oppose [Fortune's purpose], she ei-
ther kills him or she deprives him of every faculty of doing any good.*

Machiavelli is an avid player of games. When he's kicked out
of government he spends half of every day in the tavern near
his farm, gambling at cards and backgammon. Game players
spend a lot of time courting Fortune, for, with the exception of
a couple of board games (Go and chess are the clearest cases),
where the outcome depends almost entirely on skill, most
games contain a significant element of luck, and it may well
be decisive. Napoleon preferred a lucky general to a brilliant
one.

Machiavelli spends a lot of time thinking about luck and
leadership—it's one of the things that makes him the first
really modern man—and he's not happy with his conclusions.

Machiavelli very badly wants to believe that a great leader can almost always be confident about his ability to win, provided that he has studied history carefully and has mastered the lessons of brilliant advisers like Machiavelli himself. But he knows, from his own careful studies and brilliant analyses of history, and of course his experience both in government and at the card table, that some events are determined entirely by luck, not by either blunder or brilliance. When that happens, leaders, even the greatest leaders, are swept along by the tide: "Fortune thus blinds the minds of men," he ruefully tells us, "when she does not wish them to resist her designs."

Like all men of action, he goes through Houdini-like contortions to try, on the one hand, to escape this fatalistic conclusion and, on the other hand, to find a surefire way to get Lady Luck (who, out of proper respect, will henceforth be capitalized) on his side. Sometimes he acts as if Luck can be wooed and won, other times he calls for virile leaders to dominate her forcibly, bending her will to their own, and during unfortunate moments, including his own personal travails, he just shrugs his shoulders. What can you do? Anyone who has seen the amazing power of Fortune is familiar with these mental gymnastics; Machiavelli's trying to convince himself—and, even more important, trying to convince those who want to lead—that they can be the masters of their own destinies. But he knows that mastery can't be guaranteed, because Luck is more powerful than human will, and there is no known method to ensure that she will come to our side, and stay there. Her powers, and her mystery, are so great that she is capable of grand design and historic vision. She is much more than a force that determines merely a particular roll of the dice or the two remarkable bounces of ground balls over third baseman Freddy Lindstrom's head at crucial moments of the seventh game of the 1924 World Series. She is what Darth Vadar has in mind when he implores Luke Skywalker to join him to fulfill his . . . destiny.

Men of destiny know Fortune's power, even if they are sometimes reluctant to admit it. Listen to Victor Niederhoffer, a big-time currency trader, as he shorts the dollar against the yen and then watches the markets determine his destiny. Niederhoffer prides himself on his rationality, but he avidly courts Fortune when the going gets tough:

> The dollar takes my selling like I am a minnow. The dollar is pulling my house along with it.
>
> I am afraid. I have gone too far. The Japanese trend followers will all jump in if the dollar goes above 95. The bubble will drown me. The Japanese . . . run in herds. The nail that sticks out gets hammered. If the dollar sticks up any higher, the entire Japanese trading community will jump in to buy it. A higher dollar will become an ever rising bubble. . . .

Please, I beg of you. I pray: Slow down, then go down. Shame on me. How can one who has no superstition pray? . . . But the priests do not die older than others. All my praying will not make the dollar go down. . . .

The yen is my friend, and there is a full moon out. The trends often change when the moon is full. The moon affects the markets just as it affects women, crops, crime, and the tides. I am afraid I have as much chance of killing the dollar as of killing the moon. Still, I will not fail for lack of effort or preparation.[1]

But, as Machiavelli warns us, even maximum effort and intensive preparation are not sufficient to overcome Fortune when she is set on her course. On October 27, 1997, the stock market registered the biggest single-day point drop in its history. Niederhoffer bet the other way by selling highly leveraged "puts" on Standard & Poor's stock index. By the end of the day his company, Niederhoffer Global Systems, was wiped out. Its $130 million in assets had turned into $45 million in debts, for some of which he was personally liable. Had he been able to hang on for another day, he would have survived to fight on, as the market surged back some 300 points. But it was not to be; he had wagered all on the blessings of Fortune, and she rejected him. "It was like death," he said.

Even Winston Churchill, who might have been forgiven for believing that his own remarkable tenacity and courage had enabled him to lead his country to glory in its finest hour, knew that it would not have been possible without Fortune.

> I realized with awful force that no exercise of my own feeble wit and strength could save me from my enemies, and that without the assistance of that High Power which interferes in the eternal sequence of causes and effects more often than we are always prone to admit, I could never succeed.[2]

Churchill had the good fortune—aided considerably by his own exertions—to gain the cooperation of the United States, the luckiest country in the world. Mencken was of the opinion that "God protects the blind, the drunk, and the United States of America." America's great fortune begins with geographical location. Other countries have threatening neighbors; America has Mexicans and Canadians, whose greatest threats consist of cheap labor and porous borders. Fortune gives great enterprises a significant competitive advantage.

Bill Gates probably agrees. He's a game player himself, and has been all his life. Like Machiavelli, he loves card games, and he loves bridge above all others. He participates in a high-intensity contest known as the "tycoons' game," in which participation is reserved for some of the wealthiest men in America, including Warren Buffett, the Nebraska master investor who vies with Gates for the title of richest man in America. Love of bridge is common in such quarters; two of the leading bridge teams in the United States are captained by the New York investment bankers Nick Nickell and Jimmy Cayne. The latter, who is CEO of Bear Sterns, succeeded Allen "Ace" Greenberg, himself a national bridge champion. Malcolm Forbes was a bridge addict. Larry Tisch, the former owner of CBS, has played avidly throughout his adult life, and for many years participated in one of the most famous—and most expensive—afternoon games in New York City. And Ross Johnson, the former CEO of RJR Nabisco, who initiated the sequence of events that led to the leveraged buyout of his company by a group hostile to him, fought tooth and nail to get onto the posh club car that left New Canaan, Connecticut, for Manhattan every weekday morning at 7:30, so that he could play bridge with the elite of the New York business community.[3]

In an earlier generation, when the survival of the country was threatened by Hitler and fascism and our most talented people raced to public service, bridge was an integral part of the daily lives of our leaders. In the most famous bridge game in history, Generals Eisenhower and Grunther played with two other officers on a battleship in the Mediterranean, waiting for the fog to lift so that the invasion of North Africa could begin. And throughout Eisenhower's presidency, his secretary of state, John Foster Dulles, took great pride in his skill at the bridge table. Until recently, in fact, the Department of State conducted an annual worldwide bridge tournament, a legacy of that generation of great leaders. Halfway around the world, Deng Xiaoping, the man who transformed the People's Republic of China, lectured his followers: "Swimming for the body; bridge for the mind."

The reason such men love bridge—or poker, for many of the same reasons—is not only that it enables them to test their luck and skill against their peers; card games, and bridge above all others, resemble real-life competition far more than board games. In the greatest board games—chess and Go—all the pieces are seen, the balance of power is equal at the outset, and the player who best maneuvers his forces comes out the winner. In card games, each player sees only a small percentage of the cards around the table; he must discover the balance of power by listening carefully to the communications from the other players and watching their moves. In poker, or in a version of rummy that Machiavelli played in the little tavern in Sant'Andrea in Percussina, communications take the form of bets, and the "moves" have to do with drawing cards from the deck to replace discards from one's own hand, and, of course, playing the cards. Bridge is more elaborate: each player makes descriptive "bids," providing abundant information—and sometimes disinformation—to the others. Then,

during the play of the hand, defenders can provide information by their choice of card. This is why bridge is the game
closest to real life. Communication is the most important part
of the game, symbolizing all the options available to statesmen, diplomats, businessmen, and even lovers. Promises are
made and broken, and wild lies and cunning deceptions are
launched. Vital information is often withheld, while on other
occasions specific information is provided with mathematical
precision. It all depends on the situation, and on the players'
ability to grasp its reality.

Bill Gates must also be intrigued by the fact that—so far, at
least—no computer has come close to mastering bridge, even
though computers now challenge the greatest chess masters.
Gates's appreciation of the role of Luck was undoubtedly cul-
tivated at an early age, when he played bridge with his par-
ents. And it must have been greatly enhanced by the way in
which Microsoft became the most powerful software company in the world.

In the early 1980s, IBM decided to manufacture its own
personal computer and approached Microsoft for new versions of the programming languages that might be used: Basic, Fortran, Cobol, and Pascal. MS Fortran and MS Cobol
had been developed for use with Digital Research's operating
system, called CP/M; IBM decided to incorporate that operating system into the new microcomputer. IBM reps were sent

to Seattle to get signed agreements and nondisclosure statements signed by both Digital Research and Microsoft for the operating systems. Gates and his partner signed immediately, but the key Digital executive, Gary Kindall, was out of town on business, and his wife—with the full agreement of Digital's lawyers—wouldn't sign a nondisclosure agreement with IBM without her husband's explicit say-so. IBM was annoyed, and soon became even angrier. Kindall had started talks with Hewlett-Packard about providing CP/M for their new generation of computers, and he played coy with IBM, leaving for a Caribbean vacation before giving them a final answer.

IBM was in a hurry to get their new product to market, and they weren't prepared to wait any longer for Kindall. If CP/M were not going to be available, they would need a different operating system; they asked Gates if he could provide one and adapt all the Microsoft languages for use with the new operating system in less than a year. He said he could, and the deal was his.

The operating system Microsoft used was a jazzed-up version of something called the "Quick and Dirty Operating System," or QDOS. It quickly transmogrified into DOS, and Gates had it ready for IBM's deadline. Then he got lucky again: Digital was late with its new version of CP/M, thereby giving Gates a clear shot at the market with his new operating system for nearly six months. By the time the new Digital system was ready, Gates had already occupied the market, having priced DOS at 25 percent of CP/M. He was prepared to accept short-term losses to dominate the market in the long run. Finally, Gates designed DOS so that any program written in CP/M (or other competing operating systems) could easily be converted to DOS—but it was terribly difficult to convert a DOS program to CP/M.

Gates was blessed by Fortune, and then exploited his opportunity with every ounce of energy he possessed. Machiavelli says that Fortune favors the man who acts aggressively, and Gates certainly did that. He is trying to do it again now, having concluded that the next great battle for market share in the computer business will be over Internet access and navigation, and its integration with existing software.

But even such Machiavellian leaders as Gates may fail to notice when new forces appear on the battlefield. Triumphant against his commercial challengers, Gates was dealt a blow by the United States government at the end of 1997, when the Justice Department declared he had illegally violated antitrust law by making his Internet browser an inseparable part of Windows. The attack was clearly unexpected, as demonstrated by the weakness of his Washington forces. Unlike other giant American corporations, Microsoft had only token representation in the capital, and the tiny office was located in a sleepy part of town, far removed from the corridors and restaurants where the future of the nation's business is often determined. The mistake is unlikely to be repeated.

The hallmark of successful leaders is that they aggressively exploit the chances granted them by Fortune. In mid-May 1997, the soccer star Roberto Baggio was put into the lineup of the Italian national team for the first time in nineteen months. Once rated among the greatest players in the world, Baggio had slid into the limbo reserved for declining heroes. Now he had a chance to demonstrate he could still compete among the best. Five other players who were rated above him on the national charts were injured or unavailable, and there he was. Fortune then granted him an additional favor: a great pass, with two defenders and the goalie to beat. "An extraordinary goal was needed to say to the world 'I'm not finished at thirty, I still have the strength to fight, to conquer, to create beauty.'" He scored a great goal, and overnight returned to glory. As a journalistic admirer reflected the next day, "That goal reminds us to never surrender, and to nourish our dreams with faith."

Another contemporary tycoon, the flamboyant Englishman Sir James Goldsmith, was also embraced by Lady Luck at an early turning point in his career. Jimmy Goldsmith's father was the director of a French chain of luxury hotels, and he took his son along with him on tours. Young Jimmy easily and enthusiastically grew accustomed to the finer things, and along the way picked up the expected tastes for high-stakes gambling and beautiful women. With his enviable background, Goldsmith *fils* was sent to Eton for polishing. There he distinguished himself by taking no exams beyond the one required for entrance, and winning an astonishing amount of money at the race track. He graduated from Eton, and, admissions standards to the great British universities being quite flexible for candidates from families of a certain standing, he went on to Oxford for a couple of years. There he ran up a big gambling debt and had to be rescued by his father, who in desperation sent the boy into the army. This had the desired effect, and when Jimmy was discharged he was rather more disciplined, having learned to focus his ambitions on the task at hand.

His first great coup had nothing to do with business, but rather with love. He fell madly in love with Isabel, a daughter of the Bolivian multimillionaire Antenor Patino. Don Antenor was dead set against the match, for this Catholic tycoon had no intention of permitting his daughter to marry a Jewish playboy. Goldsmith managed to spirit the girl away to Scotland, where they hid for nearly a month awaiting the passage of the required time before their civil marriage could take place. Antenor fought almost to the end, until his daughter told him she was pregnant. Antenor disinherited her, and the wedding went ahead without him.

It was a short-lived triumph for Goldsmith; eight months later Isabel lapsed into a coma. The baby was delivered by cesarean, but Isabel died a few hours later.

Goldsmith now had a baby daughter—and a struggling pharmaceutical business he had taken over from his brother. He threw himself into the business with the same unrestrained passion that characterized all his activities, and within months he had built it up into a very promising enterprise. In the words of his biographer—words that could have been taken directly from Machiavelli—"The craving for expansion at any price, the rush to launch more and more on to the market, the need to keep moving at all costs, stretched their strained resources." The company was generating a lot of business but was constantly short of cash. His competitors threatened anyone who signed exclusive contracts with Goldsmith, and potential partners, sensing his weakness, offered humiliating deals to save the company. Early in July 1957 the game was up. He could not pay his bills and would have to declare bankruptcy. On a Monday morning he left his house to inform his bankers. Walking down the street he stopped at a newspaper kiosk to peruse the headlines, and saw the miraculous words BANK STRIKE. It was the first such strike in two decades, and it saved Jimmy Goldsmith from ruin. It lasted more than a week, which gave him enough time to negotiate the sale of the pharmaceutical business to his main competitor. The proceeds gave him a comfortable financial cushion, which he subsequently exploited to the utmost. But he never forgot the lesson, which Machiavelli spells out in his usual pitiless way in the *Discourses:*

> It certainly is the course of Fortune, when she wishes to effect some great result, to select for her instrument a man of such spirit and ability that he will recognize the opportunity which is afforded him. And thus, in the same way, when she wishes to effect the ruin and destruction of states, she places men at the head who contribute to and hasten such ruin.[4]

Of the latter group—leaders chosen by Fortune for their great talents for bringing on ruination—the greatest must surely be Mikhail Gorbachev, whose unique talent for destruction brought down one of history's most fearsome empires. Traditional historiography used to distinguish between "great men," those who understand their moment and impose their will on the world, and "men of providence," those through whom Fortune worked *her* will, without the actors' full understanding of what was happening. Gorbachev was just such a man; he had no intention of bringing about the fall of communism, let alone the destruction of the Soviet Empire. Gorbachev's announced goal was to save communism, not to bury it. He believed that the failure of the Soviet system was not due to the folly of central planning and the demoralization of the Soviet peoples after nearly a century of tyranny; he thought the system could be revived by giving limited political freedom, cracking down on alcoholism, and replacing the old, gray Soviet elite with more attractive and inspirational personalities like himself and his wife.

The notion of "reforming communism" was an oxymoron, and it requires a Machiavelli to explain how a man as intelligent as Gorbachev could have believed in it. Soviet communism could not be reformed. It could only be preserved by the ruthless use of terror, the method that had created it in the first place and had maintained it throughout the century. If Gorbachev was not prepared to do that, the system was doomed. But he did not understand the consequences of his actions. Indeed, as late as the failed coup in 1990, Gorbachev was still proclaiming the Soviet Communist party to be the most reliable instrument for the "reform of communism," and calling upon everyone to support it. No better example can be imagined of one who is used by Fortune to "contribute to and hasten the ruin of" a human enterprise.

Fortune does not restrict her meddling to the affairs of great men and women, and she seems to take special delight in destroying the best-laid plans of lesser lights during the course of major events. One American family in the early 1980s, convinced that the world was on the brink of thermonuclear war, spent months poring over maps and risk assessments to determine the safest place on earth, hoping to survive the impending oblivion. At last, they hit upon some small islands off the Atlantic coast of Argentina, a place so obscure and of such little value to anyone that it would be left untouched by any imaginable conflict. They sold their home, cashed in their other assets, and moved to the Falkland Islands just a few months before the Argentines invaded, kicking off the war with England.

Perhaps the most amusing example of Fortune playing practical jokes on ordinary people is the celebrated story of Major Wilmer McLean, a successful grocer from northern Virginia who found a lovely estate in Bull Run, to which he retired in 1854. Just seven years later, the armies of the Union and the Confederacy faced each other near his home, and the First Battle of Bull Run began when a Union artillery shell fell right into McLean's chimney and exploded in a kettle of stew. "The stew splattered over the room, and the luncheon menu for [General P. G. T. Beauregard, commander of the Confederate forces in the area], his staff, and the McLean household was revised."[5]

McLean decided he had chosen the wrong place for his retirement and moved the family south, to a sleepy farm in the small village of Appomattox Courthouse. It took only four years for Fortune to track him down again. As the shooting stopped on the Sunday morning of April 9, 1865, McLean was approached by a Confederate officer who was looking for a good place for Generals Lee and Grant to arrange the terms of the Confederate surrender. McLean's house was chosen, and no sooner had the documents been signed than the sack of McLean's house commenced. The table upon which Lee and Grant signed the historic documents was taken, as token "payment," by General Sheridan, and the other antiques-to-be were similarly gobbled up.

> Some officers, chiefly of cavalry, tried to buy chairs used by Lee and Grant, and when they were refused, took them off on horseback. Chairs with cane bottoms were cut up for mementoes, and the strips of cane handed out to Federals in the yard. Upholstery was cut to ribbons.[6]

At times the blessings of Fortune seem divinely inspired, as in the case of Bernard Baruch, the great American Jewish financier. In late 1901, the big shots in American industry were backing Amalgamated Copper and its effort to corner the world's copper supplies. Baruch analyzed the market, concluded that Amalgamated would fail, and instead of investing, started to "short" Amalgamated, which took nerve. The backers were annoyed with Baruch and tried to scare him off.

The key moment came in September. On Thursday the nineteenth the stock exchange closed for the funeral of President William McKinley, who had been assassinated on the sixth. The Amalgamated directors' meeting was scheduled for the next day, and the stock's immediate future would depend on whether or not they decided the company would keep paying its $8-per-share dividend. Late Friday the announcement came: the dividend had been cut by 25 percent, down to $6 per share. In those days, the stock exchange held an abbreviated session on Saturdays, and on Saturday Amalgamated dropped 7 points, closing a little above 100. The following Monday would be the day of judgment for Amalgamated's shares, and for Baruch's bet.

But Monday, as his mother reminded him on Friday, was also the day of judgment for all Jews—Yom Kippur. Baruch could not take any business decisions during that day. He told one broker to continue to short Amalgamated and took out insurance by instructing another to start buying it if it rose above a certain level. He gave instructions to all that they were not to try to reach him on Monday, whatever happened.

As it turned out, Monday, September 23, was a wild day for Amalgamated shares. The stock opened at 100 and dropped 2 points in the first hour of trading. It dropped further, then rallied to about 97 at midday, only to turn around again and dropped below 94 by the close. Baruch only learned of these events after sundown. Looking back, he said he would have gone ahead and taken his profits when the stock rallied to 97 if he had been trading that day. Instead, he now had a big profit, and considerable room for maneuver. He kept on shorting Amalgamated until it reached 60 in December. He made about $700,000 on the operation—a fortune at that time. As he wrote in his autobiography, his huge triumph was due to two things: the folly of the Amalgamated people, and "my acquiescence in my mother's request to observe a religious holiday."

Such amazing events lead Machiavelli to conclude that, whenever you see somebody who's amazingly rich, or miserably poor, go easy on the superlatives, because the odds are that "they have been brought to their ruin or their greatness by some great occasion offered by Heaven, which gives them the opportunity, or deprives them of the power, to conduct themselves with courage and wisdom." The very rich usually get that way because of some terrific stroke of luck, which, to be sure, they exploited, but the opportunity came from Fortune, not as a result of their own efforts. That is why great praise would be out of place. Similarly, the very poor should not be condemned, because they probably never had a chance. It's not your fault if you're born in the slums of Calcutta, and you're not to be praised for having a father named Rockefeller.

If luck is so important, then what good is flexibility, or for that matter any of the other skills that Machiavelli will tell you must be mastered if you are to triumph? Lady Luck can simply wipe you out, for reasons—if reasons there be—that are beyond our ken. But Machiavelli is adamant that you should not become fatalistic. First, Luck favors the intrepid, and if you master the game and pursue the proper goals with all your powers, you are more likely to gain the support of Fortune than is the lazy lout who just waits for something good to happen. Warren Buffett didn't find Fortune by lying on the couch watching TV; he constantly searches for new enterprises and even new commodities, as when he surprised the financial world by quietly accumulating one fifth of the world's silver supply. Second, you will never find out your destiny until it actually befalls you. With the exception of prophets, Fortune's intentions are not known to us, and it isn't possible to distinguish between true and false prophets until enough time passes to see if they prophesied truly or falsely. So you will have to act as if your fate is in your own hands, even though, deep down, you know that it might not be so. And if, despite all your efforts, bad luck defeats you—well, keep your sense of humor: "Not knowing the aims of Fortune, which she pursues by dark and devious ways, men should always be hopeful, and never yield to despair, whatever troubles or ill fortune may befall them."

Machiavelli hates whiners.

NATURE AND NURTURE

To be sure, we're not *entirely* in the hands of capricious fate. More often than not, the conditions under which leaders will make their life-and-death decisions are determined by human activity, and human activity can often be successfully controlled. To do that, leaders require a full understanding of the enormous variety of history. First of all, you must avoid the mistake of believing that all men are the same; there are great variations from nation to nation and sometimes even from group to group within national boundaries. Techniques of leadership must be appropriate for the specific situation.

Machiavelli knows that both nature and nurture are important in producing human behavior. He recognizes that there's an essential core common to all human beings ("Men have been . . . and ever will be, animated by the same passions, and thus they must necessarily have the same results"), but, good historian that he is, he insists that peoples are quite different from one another. "Men are more or less virtuous in one country or another, according to the nature of the education by which their manners and habits of life have been formed."[7] He is not in the least constrained by rules of political correctness, and does not hesitate to use extremely positive or negative stereotypes about entire peoples (including, above all others, his own, which he singles out for special scorn). Gnashing his teeth, he complains that the Italians have been repeatedly tricked, betrayed, and humiliated by the French and Germans, because the Italians failed to learn the basic, unsavory facts about the French and German national characters.

It's not fashionable nowadays to talk about national character, but failure to appreciate the fundamental differences among peoples can sometimes be fatal. A story famous in my college days told of a team of Madison Avenue motivators who were sent to India in the early or mid-fifties to try to get higher productivity out of the local workers at an American-owned steel mill. The owners were concerned because the Indians were leaving the shift early, and sometimes stayed away from the plant for days on end, recalling the early days of the Industrial Revolution in England, when workers stayed in the factory only until they'd earned enough money to pay their bar bills for the rest of the month. The Madison Avenue delegation divided the Indian workers into teams and created a system of rewards for the "winning" team, hoping thereby to get them to compete for the rewards, and thus work harder. But the Indians, enraged at these efforts to set them one against the other, instead threw the motivators onto the slag heap.

The Indian story shows what can happen when leaders remain ignorant of the enormous differences in national character, but there are myriad examples of successful exploitation

of the power of national character by competitors and enemies. Again in India, late in the last century, the British colo-
nial rulers came under attack from Islamic terrorists, similar
to the contemporary plague that has killed innocents from
North Africa to Israel, Lebanon, and Western Europe. The
usual forms of deterrence didn't work, because the terrorists
were convinced that the instant they died, they would ascend
to heaven with all its delights. The mere execution of the terrorists was therefore not effective, but ultimately the British
hit upon an effective solution: they buried the terrorist cadav-
ers wrapped in pigskin, thereby defiling them and barring
their passage through the heavenly gates. This inverted the relationship between terror and paradise: instead of guarantee-
ing instant entry, terrorist acts would forever prevent the
terrorists from gaining the gifts of heaven. There was a dramatic drop in terrorist activity.

Americans are particularly susceptible to the notion that all
people are fundamentally the same, and they are often led to
ruin by acting on this false assumption. The CIA, for example,
puts great stock in the polygraph, commonly known as the
"lie detector," for determining whether or not a source of information is reliable. The polygraph detects changes in body
temperature, blood pressure, and other physiological factors
as the sources are asked questions about themselves, on the
assumption that there are involuntary physiological changes if

the respondent gives false answers. But there are several groups who don't react this way, because the notion of "lying" is culture-specific. Many people respond to questions by telling the questioner what they believe he wants to hear, not what the respondent believes is "true," and such people do not necessarily feel the slightest stress while giving false answers (or, worse yet, they may undergo stress while giving truthful answers, for reasons that have nothing to do with the veracity of their response). The naive faith in the polygraph led the CIA to make some major mistakes, for example, in East Germany and Cuba during the Cold War, when virtually all the "agents" the CIA believed to be reliable turned out to be double agents. The Israelis knew better and never invested the polygraph with the near-magical qualities the Americans ascribed to it. They had learned early on that the device didn't work at all with the local Bedouins, and they reasoned that if it failed with one group it was necessarily suspect in other cases as well.

Even if leaders are knowledgeable about national and cultural differences, there is no guarantee of success, because there are problems that baffle certain kinds of leaders, no matter how well they prepare for their challenges. Different leaders have different personalities with different inclinations and impulses, and a leader's destiny is determined by the interplay between his personality and the nature of the challenges he encounters. "Times and affairs . . . change often, and as men do not change their imaginations and their procedures, it happens that a man at one time has good fortune and at another bad." Successful leaders require profound insight into the nature of the historic moment in which they are operating.

THE TENOR OF THE TIMES

Machiavelli is not the kind of historian who believes that you can explain events by laying out a series of casual links. He is more of the Chinese school, holding that one should analyze historical events by studying the unique characteristics of a given moment, or period. "That man is fortunate who harmonizes his procedure with his time," and a man is unlucky indeed when he is out of synch. We're all familiar with the sort who metaphorically beats his head against a stone wall, continuing on a course of action long after it has been demonstrated to be a loser. That person is out of harmony with the moment. Steve Jobs, the eccentric creator of Apple Computers, drove the company to the verge of ruin, all the while insisting that the world would eventually realize that he had been right all along and would stop buying IBM-compatibles in favor of Apples, Lisas, and Macs. Jobs had great talent, but he did not recognize that he was out of synch with the market. Apple was fortunate to survive.

Pope John Paul II holds the same sort of view of history as Machiavelli. Shortly after his accession to the papacy, he explained to his close collaborators in the Vatican that there were moments when even the bravest person could have little effect on the world, because powerful forces were driving human events in a certain direction. But there were other moments when single individuals could have amazing impact, and the pope believed that his papacy was one such moment. He therefore undertook to inspire, cajole, and provoke people all over the world to take action. His slogan, "Be not afraid," reflected the Polish pope's conviction that the time was ripe for heroic individuals. The fall of the Soviet Empire was due in no small part to John Paul II's keen understanding of the historical moment.

Ronald Reagan also understood that the Evil Empire's moment had come, and said so in a speech to the British Parliament in 1981, but there was such disdain for Reagan by the Western intelligentsia that most students of the Cold War continue to repeat the false claim that "virtually nobody foresaw the collapse of the Soviet Union." Both Reagan and the pope understood that its fall could be accomplished, and both worked to make it come about.

Obviously, both were well suited to the task and were in great harmony with their times, while their critics and opponents—those who believed the Soviet Empire was destined to win the Cold War, and those who thought the Soviet system was at least as stable as the democratic West—were out of synch. Right up to the end, the West Germans paid hard cash to the East German regime for every German who was permitted to emigrate from East to West, and Israel paid off the Romanians for the trickle of Jews who came out from Ceauşescu's harsh tyranny. Both could have saved a lot of money.

Understanding the uniqueness of the moment enables you to rule effectively, not only because you will be able to grasp the opportunities at hand, but also because you will appreciate the requirements of your own enterprise. Machiavelli compares political rule with the proper care of the human body: "All worldly things have a limit on their lives; but those fulfill their days as ordained by heaven that do not damage their body, but keep it in good order."[8]

All organizations, from business to athletic teams, from states to religions, public or private, large or small, have a natural life cycle, and just as we can shorten or prolong our own lives by paying attention to the rules of good health, so organizations live longer if they are properly constituted and well managed. Each has a set of rules that work best, and the rules vary both according to the kind of organization and to its stage of life.

Most of the conventional wisdom about leadership is dangerously wrong, because it suggests that there is a set of unchanging principles which, if applied diligently, always give the best chance of success. Machiavelli rejects this. Methods that work in one set of circumstances are disastrous in another setting. Different problems, different contexts, require different methods. Ichak Adizes, one of our most creative business thinkers, could be paraphrasing Machiavelli when he says: "There are no absolute solutions. It all depends. What is right and what is wrong depends on what needs to be done and how."[9]

You cannot dominate Fortune, but you must act as if your own actions are going to be decisive. You must understand the great variety of human nature, and fully grasp the uniqueness of the historical moment and the nature of the enterprise you command. And one more thing: know that, should you triumph, your troubles are only just beginning.

CHAPTER THREE

THE WAR OF POLITICS

It is easy to persuade them of a thing, but it is difficult to keep them in that persuasion.

The Prussian general Carl von Clausewitz famously wrote that war is the continuation of politics by other means, and the reverse is equally true. In many parts of the world, even today, political losers pay with their lives just as surely as if they had been killed on the battlefield. In these conflicts, as in those in more civilized societies, where defeat means only loss of position or prestige, the winner owes much to the behavior of those who fight for, or alongside, him. It is easy to understand why a person would fight to the death to defend his own life, or family, or farm, or home, but no one is born with the desire to risk his life or even his career for company, team, or country.

Many philosophers believe that man is a political and social animal, for whom it is altogether natural to associate with his fellows and make common cause. Not Machiavelli. "There is no hidden hand which brings all these human activities into natural harmony," as Isaiah Berlin puts it.[1] In Machiavelli's world—the real world as described in the truthful history books—treason and deceit are commonplace, as are conspiracies against constituted authority, all undertaken for personal satisfaction, like that which comes from dominating, not harmoniously working with, others. Think of the past few years' stories out of Central and East Africa: Hutus slaughter half a million Tutsis in ninety days, and millions of Tutsi refugees panic and run, producing misery, disease, and mass death from starvation. Aid arrives, the situation briefly stabilizes, and then reverses: the Tutsis, supported by fellow tribesmen from the marauding forces of Zairean insurrectionaries, now slaughter Hutus, who panic and run, producing even more misery, disease, and mass death from starvation.

Forget all that cheerful talk about spontaneous association. "All men are wicked," Machiavelli tells us with dramatic overstatement early in the *Discourses,* and "they will always give vent to the malignity that is in their minds when opportunity offers." Human wickedness brings men and their creations to ruin. As Europe headed into the darkness of the fascist era, Winston Churchill glumly scribbled an outline for a melancholy speech.

What a terrible disappointment the Twentieth Century

has been

How terrible & how melancholy

is long series of disastrous events

wh have darkened its first 20 years.

We have seen in ev country a dissolution,

a weakening of those bonds,

a challenge to those principles

a decay of faith

an abridgment of hope

on wh structure & ultimate existence

of civilized society depends.

We have seen in ev part of the globe

one gt country after another

wh had erected an orderly, a peaceful

a prosperous structure of civilized society,

relapsing in hideous succession

into bankruptcy, barbarism or anarchy.

To get people to work together, let alone risk their lives for a
common enterprise, requires work: tough, dirty, nasty work—

the work of leaders. You cannot count on human beings to spontaneously or voluntarily do the right thing, because their instincts run in the opposite direction. As the protagonist of Robert Penn Warren's novel *All the King's Men* tells an idealistic associate, "Goodness. Yeah, just plain, simple goodness. Well you can't inherit that from anybody. You got to make it out of badness. . . . And you know why? Because there isn't anything else to make it out of."[2]

And that's only the half of it. Mankind, as the American novelist Stanley Elkin once remarked, can be divided into two rough categories, the livers and the let-livers. Machiavelli is decidedly a liver, sometimes even a high-liver. His letters, like his days and nights, are full of lively sexual activity, and he is the life of many a party. Writing to a friend, he remarks that anybody reading their letters would at first think they were "grave men, wholly concerned with important matters," but then, reading further along, would discover that "we, the very same persons, were light minded, inconstant, lascivious, concerned with empty things." He finds this thoroughly natural, even though some would be inclined to criticize them for giving in to lust and frivolousness. "We are imitating Nature, who is variable; and he who imitates her cannot be blamed."

Alas, this element of human nature poses a grave problem for leaders. While it may be quite natural for men to indulge their sensual desires, the insatiable quest for pleasure quickly causes imbalance, overwhelming judgment just as surely, and just as ruinously, as the unbridled quest for more wealth and power. Machiavelli, who falls in love often and enthusiastically, knows well that one cannot reason effectively with someone in passionate pursuit of his beloved. Even the toughest military man can have his will undone by a dazzling woman. When Italian troops were left untouched in Lebanon in 1983 while other allied forces were repeatedly subjected to sniper fire and terrorist attacks, many wondered how the Italians had managed to avoid casualties. Fifteen years later it was revealed that the Syrian defense minister had ordered the Lebanese to leave the Italians alone because he had a lifelong crush on the movie star Gina Lollobrigida. General Mustafa Tlass told an interviewer from the Dubai newspaper *Al-Bayan,* "I gathered the Lebanese resistance leaders together and told them: do whatever you want with the U.S., British, and other forces, but I do not want a single Italian soldier to be hurt. . . . I do not want a single tear falling from the eyes of Gina Lollobrigida. . . . I used to collect her pictures and send her letters from the frontline or any other place in the world."[3]

When Tlass became chief of staff, in 1968, Lollobrigida began answering his letters, and he sent her books, jewelry, and antiques. At his repeated urging, she returned the favor by visiting him in Damascus, cementing the friendship at a family banquet. Machiavelli knows that a man in the grips of such passion cannot be expected to exercise iron self-discipline. He will continue the pursuit of his beloved. Having been overcome by the same emotions, Machiavelli accepts the inevitable. He agrees with Boccaccio "that it is better to do and regret than not to do and regret," even when it makes life very difficult. Writing of an affair with a local woman, he confesses: "Everything seems easy to me, and to [her] every desire, no matter how different to that which should be mine, I conform. And though I seem to have entered great trouble, yet I feel in it such sweetness."[4]

His desire overwhelms even his dedication to his work: "No longer do I delight in reading about the deeds of the ancients or in discussing those of the moderns; everything has been transformed into tender thoughts, for which I thank Venus."

The desire for more drives us wildly after pleasures of all sorts: food, sex, narcotics, alcohol, music. (Tobacco had barely arrived in Renaissance Italy; the rich and powerful cigars that bear the name of Tuscany are of later vintage.) Our sensual desires are vast, and are never far from our attention, even when we are dealing with the most profound subjects. It's hard to stay focused, because temptation is all around us. In the throes of passion or the mire of self-indulgence or the sweet lethargy of indolence, man pays little heed to moral sermons or standards of good conduct. He will do anything—lie, cheat, steal, rape, kill—to satisfy his urges. No family, no business, and surely no nation or army can long withstand such a degradation of its component parts.

Here is a new threat. Not only are we menaced by enemies within and without, eager to remove us from power, take our riches, and dominate us, but we are all too eager to do ourselves in. Men are not only ambitious but also lazy, slothful, arrogant, dissolute, and self-indulgent. Machiavelli knows the moral gutter well, for he's surrounded by it, and in his weaker moments sinks into it. In one of his letters he speaks of Florence as "a magnet for all the imposters of the world." These characteristics are as much a piece of human nature as the passion for power and domination, but they lead in the opposite direction. Ambition takes us up, to build new institutions, create and accumulate more wealth, expand our domination, and thereby make possible new countries, even empires. Once we reach one pinnacle, however, the spoils of victory erode our passion for more, and lead us into the paths of temptation. We are happy to succumb. Indolence, sloth, greed, and the other self-centered sins and vices lead downward to disintegration, internal discord, and domination by others. The language tells us which is easier (as if we didn't know): the climb up the hill of success is hard work, while the slide into the muck requires little effort. History's garbage bin is full to overflowing with men, enterprises, nations, and empires that achieved great success through years, decades, even centuries, of great effort, only to rot from within, making them easy prey to their enemies. Sometimes the enemy isn't even necessary; the rottenness is sufficient to produce ruin all by itself.

Machiavelli puts it all into one of his neat epigrams about the constant turning of the historical wheel: "Virtue breeds quiet, quiet indolence, indolence disorder, disorder ruin; and similarly out of ruin order is born, from order virtue, out of this glory and good fortune."[5]

The Perils of Victory

Your troubles don't end when you make it to the top; indeed, they actually multiply. You will have to worry about your own rotten instincts and those of your people, as well as about enemies and competitors. Two wars have to be waged, one against those trying to do you in, using the real weapons of the battlefield or the figurative ones common in political, athletic, or business competition; the other, just as dramatic, against your own worst impulses. The greater your success in the first, which makes you stronger and richer, the greater your peril in the second—as your wealth and power provoke the ruinous tendencies of your nature. Not that there are no good men; there are, but they are not players in this drama. They don't threaten your rise, or participate in your fall. Their virtue, unlike yours, is its own reward. You only have to worry about the men and women you find on the battlefield, or those that drag you over the edge, and they are fighting for quite different rewards.

The best chance to triumph on the battlefield and resist the seductions of indolence and self-indulgence lies in virtue and discipline, the qualities of good soldiers. "A prince," Machiavelli warns, "must have no other objective or other thought or take anything for his craft, except war,"[6] meaning that the virtues of the warrior are those of all great leaders of any successful organization. It is often said that people don't want to be governed by military men in peacetime, but that is only half true. The examples of de Gaulle and Eisenhower show that a certain kind of military leader can become an equally great political figure. The people don't want to be governed by military men who aren't able to adapt to peacetime. John Keegan has written perhaps the best description of what it is about military heroes that worries civil society:

In all societies there are men who are good at war and cannot be anything but soldiers. I was writing such a man's obituary the other day. I knew him well. . . . Having seen him depart, bayonet fixed, at the head of an attack, and seen him return, bloodstained and satiated, they identified, not with his bravery but with the terror he must have aroused in those he met—for the brief moment they still lived. Indeed, bravery does not describe his quality. He simply did not feel the same emotions as others do in the face of death. Death was something he gave, not received, and because his powers of giving were so much greater than those of anyone he was likely to meet, fear did not inhabit his person.[7]

We want this kind of leader when we have to fight evil enemies, but we don't want him in charge of civil society. On the other hand, a leader who can fight evil enemies and take charge of civil society, changing his style and methods to suit the circumstances, can achieve unique results. Indeed, as Machiavelli insists, a truly great political leader must be capable of using military power. Margaret Thatcher demonstrated that in the Falklands War, and it is surely no accident that America's Founding Father, George Washington, and perhaps her greatest president, Abraham Lincoln, demonstrated greatness in both war and peacetime. Most countries owe their creation and continued existence to victory in war.

Preparing for war makes you tough, and reminds you of the qualities necessary for victory: cold, prudent judgment, alertness to changing conditions, bravery under fire, courage when challenged, solidarity with your comrades-at-arms, and total commitment to mission. Such preparation is physically and mentally taxing, leaving little time or energy for the enjoyment of luxury. Furthermore, the good warrior is dedicated to advancing the common cause ("the corps, the corps" as MacArthur intoned in his elegant farewell speech), not his own personal situation. The force of arms goes hand in hand with good laws and good leadership to maintain a sound and secure nation, for domestic men-at-arms—police and militias in their various forms—enforce the laws and uphold the power of the state. But Machiavelli is adamant that might alone does not make right. Without good laws, there can be no good arms, for they would be employed to advance an illegitimate cause.

Like war itself, military preparation provides a real test of character, and in the best circumstances creates a pool of leaders for the nation. "In what man ought the country to find greater faith than in he who has to promise to die for her?" Machiavelli asks rhetorically, and we have generally done quite well when we followed this advice. Ulysses Grant and the military hero William Henry Harrison were not great presidents, but America had moments of real glory under the leadership of George Washington, Theodore Roosevelt, and Dwight Eisenhower, all advocates of manly vigor, moral rigor, and prudence in the conduct of our national affairs. All became political leaders in large part because of the heroic qualities they demonstrated in wartime, and to those who like to believe that such men would have become great national figures in more tranquil times, Machiavelli shakes his head. "It has always been, and always will be, that great and rare men in a republic are neglected in peacetime." This is "times make the man" with a vengeance: great men are esteemed and elevated in difficult times, and sent out to pasture once victory is achieved. Ask Winston Churchill or Charles de Gaulle, or those tough corporate turnaround specialists who save floundering enterprises by cutting back to the bone, drilling the survivors to carry out the new mission, and taking back market share inch by bloody inch.

Thus, paradoxically, peace increases our peril, by making discipline less urgent, encouraging some of our worst instincts, and depriving us of some of our best leaders. The great Prussian general Helmuth von Moltke knew whereof he spoke when he wrote a friend, "Everlasting peace is a dream, not even a pleasant one; war is a necessary part of God's arrangement of the world. . . . Without war the world would deteriorate into materialism."[8] As usual, Machiavelli dots the *i*'s and crosses the *t*'s: it's not just that peace undermines discipline and thereby gives the destructive vices greater sway. If we actually achieved peace, "Indolence would either make [the state] effeminate or shatter her unity; and the two things together, or each by itself, would be the cause of her ruin."[9] This is Machiavelli's variation on a theme by Mitterrand: the absence of movement is the beginning of defeat.

71

Machiavelli uses the word "effeminate" to describe a weak and indecisive leader or organization, but he certainly knows that women are as capable of strong and coherent leadership as men are. Indeed, he ranks some female rulers on a par with the best men, and he has a special soft spot for a Renaissance personnage, the "Madonna of Forli." Madonna Caterina fell into the clutches of her enemies. They killed her husband, captured her and the children, and then demanded she give them control of the city fortress. De Grazia completes the spellbinding tale:

> Promising her captors that if they let her go in, she would induce [the guard of the fortress] to open up, Madonna Caterina left her children behind as hostages. Once inside, she appeared on the walls, spat on the assassins, threatened them with fearful revenge, and, crying out that she still retained the means to make other children, she raised her skirts and showed them her genitals. The conspirators fled.[10]

Don't underestimate the strength of women! Machiavelli knows they are anything but passive. Indeed, he reserves special scorn for anyone stupid enough to get on the wrong side of a woman, for he's likely to pay a terrible price for his idiocy.

The one who offends woman
Wrongly or rightly is mad if he believes
through prayers and weeping to find mercy in her.
As she descends in this mortal life,
with her soul she brings along
pride, haughtiness, and of pardon none;
trickery and cruelty accompany her
and give her such help
that each enterprise increases her desire;
and if contempt bitter and ugly
moves her or jealousy, she acts and handles it:
and her strength exceeds mortal strength.[11]

Like Machiavelli, we know that women can be tough. Women can command states and armies—as the military rulers of Argentina became painfully aware when they tangled with Margaret Thatcher over the Falklands, and the Arab leaders, when they tried to destroy Israel during the premiership of Golda Meir—and they can also fight, especially working solo, like flying certain kinds of aircraft or using small arms in unconventional situations. Women have been outstanding terrorists, from the Japanese Red Army to the Italian Red Brigades to the German Baader-Meinhof Group, one of whose cofounders was Ulrike Meinhof, later convicted of murder. The Italian prime minister Aldo Moro was executed by a lady terrorist, and a planeful of oil ministers was hijacked in Vienna in the mid-seventies by a terrorist group led by an Arab woman, Leila Khaled. Women have performed heroically in special forces and from Delilah to Mata Hari have famously been exceptional espionage agents.

On the other hand, Machiavelli insists that the differences between the sexes are so great as to impose different obligations on men and women. First of all, Machiavelli believes that women are not nearly so prone to evil as men. The protection of women is therefore a moral imperative, and Machiavelli warns would-be princes that one of the most dangerous acts they can undertake is to violate their subjects' women. Furthermore, while women can be as psychologically tough as men, they can't match men's physical prowess. Women like Margaret Thatcher, Golda Meir, and Indira Gandhi have equaled men's performances on the symbolic battlefields of politics, but they would lose in the literal combat of war itself. There is no contest between men and women in physical battle. Strength, speed, stamina—the prime ingredients of the good fighter—favor men by a very wide margin. Moreover, women do not seek fulfillment in military service as eagerly as men do; in the United States armed forces, where each military service must fill a female quota, it costs half again as much to recruit a woman as to recruit a man. With rare exceptions, women cannot achieve military glory as men do, because they almost always lack the physical wherewithal and the passionate desire to achieve it. That is one sense in which Machiavelli describes a feeble or irresolute state and its weak-kneed leaders as effeminate.

There is an additional resonance to "effeminate," flowing from the fact that the presence of women around an army is invariably a source of disruption, a potentially dangerous breakdown in discipline and morale. When Machiavelli was in charge of a military force, he banished women—including the inevitable camp followers—from the immediate environs. Only in this way could he ensure that his fighting men would concentrate entirely on the task at hand. Patton, in like manner, forbade even pinups during World War II. Women are a distraction to men, as are the other temptations that weaken resolve, sap energies, and corrupt judgment. In Machiavelli's lexicon, an effeminate state or organization is one in which the slide into indolence and self-indulgence is under way. Such a state has turned away from the virtues of good arms and good laws, leading to the almost certain ruin of the common good. The corruption of the leaders threatens the strength and success of the entire undertaking, because corrupt leaders lack the discipline and the dedication to mission without which no organization can win.

CLINTON'S AMERICA:
CORRUPTION AND CONTEMPT

In *The Art of War,* Machiavelli describes a generation of Italian leaders just before they were crushed by ambitious foreign invaders:

> They thought . . . that it sufficed for a prince in the writing-rooms of palaces to think up a sharp reply, to write a beautiful letter, to demonstrate wit and readiness in saying and words, to know how to weave a fraud . . . to keep many lascivious women around, to conduct himself avariciously and proudly, to rot in idleness, to give military rank by favor, to be scornful if anyone might show them any praiseworthy path, to want their words to be oracular responses, nor did these no-accounts realize that they were preparing themselves to be the prey of whoever assaulted them.[12]

Anyone looking closely at Bill Clinton's America will be struck by the clinical accuracy with which Machiavelli has described this president and the intimate relationship between his personal corruption and his rejection of military virtue. Clinton combines a passionate frenzy for self-satisfaction, verging on obsessive and compulsive sexual behavior,[13] with lifelong contempt for the military, whose total devotion to the common good is the opposite of his own. The U.S. Marines instill this devotion in their recruits from the first minutes of basic training on Parris Island: "Stenciled on the pillars flanking Staff Sergeant Rowland in black and red letters are the words CORE VALUES: HONOR. COURAGE. COMMITMENT. ('These are things,' explains former Marine Commandant Al Gray, 'that come before the self.')"[14]

Most contemporary leaders—Clinton may be an extreme case, but he is hardly unique—are little interested in "things that come before the self." Machiavelli brilliantly exposes the connection between such leaders' self-indulgence and their inability to craft effective strategy. Their passion for self-fulfillment leaves little mental and emotional space for the common good, and they are consequently unable to coherently use power against their enemies. Such self-indulgent princes are extremely reluctant to send armies into the field. Even when Clinton felt he must do so, as in Iraq, he ordered his generals to avoid casualties, and therefore any hope of victory. The corrupt princes that so enrage Machiavelli feared danger, and therefore "removed themselves from the army," just as Clinton did when he used all his cunning to avoid military service during the Vietnam War. Such leaders use military power to enhance their image, not to advance the common good. We have already heard Machiavelli sadly observe, "If we occasionally see a king go to war himself . . . it is done for the sake of pomp only, and not from any praise-worthy motive."[15] It's a photo-op, not virtue.

Clinton both feared war, and recognized that it was impor-tant for the American people to believe he was a warrior. The *Washington Post* revealed on August 27, 1998, that the Clin-ton administration had been secretly cancelling United Na-tions inspections in Iraq ever since the previous fall, despite mobilizing the armed forces and publicly threatening harsh reprisals if Saddam Hussein failed to agree to the inspections. Secretary of State Madeleine Albright railed at accusations of timidity, arguing, according to the *Post,* that she and her col-leagues were trying "only to control the pace of confrontation with Iraq to create the best conditions in which to prevail." In simple English, since Clinton was neither ready nor able to mount a serious threat to Saddam's regime, he ran from a con-flict that would expose American impotence. When the chief American inspector, Scott Ritter, resigned in disgust over this duplicitous policy, he was savagely attacked by the adminis-tration, and then investigated for leaking classified material to the public.

The Iraq fiasco was not exceptional, as is demonstrated by the other major deployment of American armed forces during Clinton's presidency: Bosnia. The mission in Bosnia was quite different from the Iraq one, as the latter was intended as a reprisal for aggression while the former was defined as a "peacekeeping" operation. But, as in Iraq, there was a concern verging on obsession with the possibility of American casualties. Massive intelligence resources were diverted to Bosnia, so that we would get advance warning of any hostile actions against our people. Such concern may seem laudable in the abstract, but so much attention was paid to Bosnia—surveillance satellites were diverted to provide constant coverage—that we had much less information from areas where war was a real possibility, such as Korea and Taiwan, during the run-up to the elections in early summer, 1996. As in Iraq, American commanders were instructed to avoid the most remote possibility of fighting with the enemy, which had the effect of providing an enhanced degree of security to several indicted "war criminals," thereby making long-term stability in the area less likely. Such long-term concerns—the sort that should be taken seriously if leaders are truly concerned with national security—were overwhelmed by the fear of the political consequences of American casualties.

This kind of corruption of the national mission, combined with the myth that peace is normal, produces a solvent strong enough to dissolve the strength of our armed forces and the integrity of our political and military leaders. The supreme importance of the military and the morale that binds fighting men together derive from the recognition that, without them, our enemies will kill or dominate us. If our leaders, not believing that our survival depends on our ability to win the next war, devote their energies to avoiding news of casualties, the armed forces become just another social institution, and even a laboratory for experimentation: for example, placing women alongside men in combat units. The Israeli military historian Martin Van Creveld, testifying before a presidential commission on women in the armed forces, compared the American attitude with that in his own country:

> For us, the military are a question of survival. . . . For you, the military is not a question, and for over a century, actually since your Civil War . . . has never been a question of life and death. It has always been a question of "shall we or shan't we? Can we or can't we?" . . .
>
> So you can afford to make all kinds of . . . what I must say to outsiders often appear like bizarre social experiments, because it doesn't matter anyhow. . . . The very fact that you have this debate may itself be construed as proof that it's not serious. It's a game. It's a joke.

The corruption that Machiavelli knows and understands so well has penetrated the American armed forces to the point where military leaders are constantly forced to redefine "success" in order to meet the criteria of the "bizarre social experiments" their political superiors have ordered. Women are unable to meet the same physical standards as men, but instead of limiting women's roles, the standards have been systematically diluted. If proper standards were enforced, only a handful of women would graduate from flight school and win their pilot's wings, but since there is a political requirement for more women, the standards have accordingly been eased. A carrier crew must be able to evacuate their wounded on stretchers in case of emergency, but two women cannot manage a stretcher with a man on it. The stretchers have therefore been redesigned for four carriers, and the evacuation task has been redefined as a "four-person" exercise. Officers who refuse to compromise standards so as to make it appear as if women were really physically competitive with men are directed to take early retirement. Meanwhile, a new generation of navy ships is now on the drawing boards, and will include wider sink drains (for longer female hair), stronger exhaust fans (to get rid of hair-spray fumes), gentler washing machines, and so forth. And, since there are so many pregnant women on board, ships must now meet safety requirements for fetuses, such as noise and temperature levels.

The corruption of standards is grave indeed, but perhaps not so grave as the demoralization (in the fullest sense of the term) of the armed forces produced by constant close contact between men and women. Anyone who manages a large organization knows how difficult it is to eliminate sexual attraction from working relationships. The business community, after years of attempting to ban office romances, finally yielded to the inevitable in early 1998: "Instead of trying to ban managers dating subordinates, many major companies are now changing the rules to accommodate them. . . . 'Trying to outlaw romance is like trying to outlaw the weather,' an IBM executive told the *Wall Street Journal*."[16]

If it has proved impossible to separate sex from mission in American corporations, it is far more difficult and damaging to attempt to do so in the armed forces. The disruptive problems are increased by orders of magnitude when, as is now the case, young men and women are put side by side under enormously stressful conditions like basic training or extended sea duty. The passions, frustrations, and jealousies are devastating to the creation of a disciplined and selfless military, where the common good is so important that every soldier must be prepared to sacrifice everything, including life itself, to defend it. It's hard enough to convince a man that he should be willing to die for his country when he's surrounded by like-minded men and is subjected to iron discipline and exhausting physical training, without subverting discipline and morale by tempting him with opportunities for sex.

The Israelis, whose armed forces some consider the best in the world, not least because of their exceptional morale, take great care to segregate the sexes. Women are not under male command, nor, in the event of disciplinary procedures, are they judged by men or treated by male doctors. In an emergency, if no female doctor can be found, another woman attends during treatment by a male. Women serve in female units and are kept away from the combat zone. Separate because unequal, the women are nonetheless highly esteemed and protected. In contrast, American forces in Bosnia initially had co-ed tents—and a pregnancy rate well above the servicewide average. Local media acidly commented that the army troops were too busy breeding to capture war criminals. Morale was so badly disrupted that the sexes had to be separated, confirming Machiavelli's view of the matter.

The fatal connection between abandoning military standards and the corruption of civic virtue is demonstrated by the argument now advanced by those who want to expand women's military roles: they say that there are not enough qualified men available to fill the billets, and so we need women. The shortage of men shows that military service has lost its traditional prestige, which for Machiavelli is a fatal sign of the corruption of proper values. In Machiavelli's virtuous state, military service is considered an honor and an obligation, and Machiavellian leaders insist that men carry out their duties. Until the mass protest against the Vietnam War in the mid-1970s, all American men were liable to serve two

years in the military, but the military draft was eliminated by
Richard Nixon in order to defuse the political protest of the
privileged classes. There was a brief revival of military prestige in the years of our victories in the Cold War (in no small
part because we thwarted the Soviets and their proxies in
battle in Angola, Grenada, and Afghanistan) and the Gulf War,
flawed though it was. But, as always, victory led to corruption, with the results Machiavelli describes so well.

Simple prudence dictates that we should maintain our considerable military advantage vis-à-vis potential enemies, especially at a time of diminished military investment and a
shrinking military sector in American science and industry.
Instead, we have done the opposite. During the Bush and
Clinton presidencies we have provided the Chinese with some
of our best military technology, much of it at bargain-
basement prices. We have sold them the crucial "hot section"
technology that gives modern aircraft engines their special
thrust, thereby ensuring that the next generation of Chinese
fighter aircraft will have the world's best engines. We have
sold them dangerously large quantities of supercomputers, the
spinal cord of modern warfare. In a fifteen-month period from
late 1995 to early 1997, the Clinton administration approved
the sale of forty-six supercomputers, which is more than those
currently in use in the Pentagon, the military services, and the
intelligence community combined. This will enormously help
the Chinese design advanced weapons, including weapons of

mass destruction, as well as aircraft and missiles, and it will enable them to make a quantum leap in their ability to encrypt their own communications and decipher ours. We have permitted them to purchase advanced machine tools to build wings for fighter planes and the highly refined "skin" for ballistic missiles; the manufacturing know-how for the Global Positioning System, which they can use to give their cruise missiles lethal accuracy; small jet engines, for the same cruise missiles; and laboratories for testing "stealth" technology. And this is only a part of a long list.

As these facts emerged, the Clinton administration repeatedly denied any laws had been broken (as if this were the issue), and continued about its business virtually unchallenged by Congress or the major media. The actions were, in Talleyrand's elegant phrase, "worse than a crime . . . a blunder" and they were done in such a way as to avoid any public debate. The "hot section" technology, for example, had long been embargoed to hostile or potentially hostile countries, and all advanced military technology had been denied to China by law ever since the Tiananmen Square massacre. Clinton quietly redefined the technology, removed it from the list of sensitive military items, and transferred authority for licensing from the State Department to the Commerce Department, where his friend Ron Brown quickly approved the deal.

The supercomputer scheme followed a similar pattern. We have long had an agreement with Japan, the only other country to manufacture effective supercomputers, to restrict super-computer sales outside the West, precisely because of their military significance. First, Clinton redefined the supercomputer category, unilaterally raising the ceiling for allowable computing power more than thirty times, over the violent objections of some of our closest European allies, then proclaimed that the redefined computers were for "civilian" use, thereby giving the Commerce Department authority to approve the sales. Secretary of State Madeleine Albright maintained the fiction when stories surfaced in the early summer of 1997 that American supercomputers had been found hard at work at Chinese military installations. She said she was confident they were being used for civilian purposes, but how could she know? Even the Pentagon experts charged with monitoring such exports didn't know the licenses had been issued until a Commerce Department official revealed it in testimony to a House oversight committee late in the spring.

The issue of arming China is fundamental to our very survival. The worst possible scenario for American survival would be a hostile China, with the biggest army in the world, armed with the finest weapons *our* technology can produce. Thanks to two successive administrations, this scenario is now conceivable. It is hard to imagine a more dramatic example of Machiavelli's warning that indolent and corrupt leadership threatens the very existence of the nation. It is not only the "moral fiber" of the nation that is threatened by corruption, as many moralists imagine, but also its ability to defend its interests throughout the world and, in the end, its very survival.

It is comforting to believe, as many do, that great wealth can be an adequate substitute for military power. When the Cold War ended, it was widely proclaimed that the conflicts of the future would be commercial, not military, and that the winners of the wars of the future would be the wealthy rather than the powerful. Machiavellian leaders do not accept such reassurances, having learned that "men, steel, money and bread are the sinews of war; but of these four, the first two are more important, because men and steel find gold and bread, but bread and gold do not find men and steel."[17] In fact, weak and wealthy is the worst of all, because the wealth will attract the attention of those with the will and the power to take it from us. Rome was conquered by barbarians, after all.

CHAPTER FOUR

OF GOOD AND EVIL

HAMLET: What news?
ROSENCRANTZ: None, my lord, but that the world's
grown honest.
HAMLET: Then is doomsday near.

Not a pretty picture is it? Driven by ambition and the desires
of the flesh, unconstrained by any political or social instinct,
unguided by a hidden hand, we humans claw for wealth and
power. Once victorious, we degenerate, leaving our conquests
and acquisitions open to domination by others or disintegration caused by the rot within. Rising or falling, human passion
easily overwhelms reason, making men and women behave
no better than animals.

Left to our own devices we will *not* recreate Pericles' *polis;*
we will spawn Liberia, Zaire, Bosnia, and Cambodia, the Cultural Revolution, Auschwitz, and the Gulag Archipelago.

Federico Fellini's little masterpiece, *The Orchestra Re-*

hearsal, tells us about the human instinct for ruin, even in— or especially in—the most sensitive and talented people. In the film, a guest conductor arrives for a rehearsal and finds the players in an ornery mood. "Who is he to tell *us* how to play?" they ask. They have played this piece a thousand times! If only they were free to play as they wish, instead of the way he demands, the performance would be far better. Is art not enhanced by free creativity? Is not the authoritarian conductor suppressing their freedom of expression? They rebel against the conductor, driving him from the podium. Independence at last! But when they start rehearsing by themselves, it's chaos, and the chaos soon degenerates into a free-for-all. Musicians are injured, instruments destroyed. In the end they beg the conductor to come back. This time he counts out the tempo in German, and there is no more nonsense from the orchestra. Just as in Machiavelli's political fairy tale, democracy degenerates into anarchy, which opens the door to the tyrant.

Leave us to our own devices, and all hell breaks loose. Give us total freedom, and we will reenact *The Lord of the Flies.* We are "more ready for evil than for good." Therefore, we must *not* be left to our own devices. We must be forced or, under ideal circumstances, convinced or inspired to do good. This can be done (that, too, is in the history books), and the results have been spectacular. Properly led, we can achieve glory. But the task is hard and never-ending, for we must overcome our own ruinous impulses as well as thwart those who seek to dominate us for their own satisfaction. And since we will do anything to satisfy our ruinous impulses, all manner of nastiness may be required to keep us under control, and to defeat our enemies.

There's the rub: In order to achieve the most noble accomplishments, the leader may have to "enter into evil." This is the chilling insight that has made Machiavelli so feared, admired, and challenging. It is why we are drawn to him still, half a millennium later, like moths to the killer flame. We are rotten, it's true, but we can achieve greatness if, and only if, we are properly led. We are prey for our fellow men, yet with great leaders we can prevail. But those who undertake to lead us to glory are going to be in for a hell of a fight, no holds barred.

If you're not prepared to fight without quarter, don't play this game. "Prophets who came with arms were successful, while those who were not armed were ruined."[1] The road to hell is littered with the corpses of the well meaning; Machiavelli expects his leaders to be serious. If you want to lead, you must demonstrate your ability to rule your own people and defeat your enemies, and the only way is to show your power. You "must presuppose all men criminal, and that they will always use the malignity of their spirit whenever they may have free occasion."[2] Any sign of weakness invites attack. Lyndon Johnson, when asked how he intended to win the struggle for the hearts and minds of the Congress at a particularly difficult moment, responded with a fine Machiavellian quip: "When you've got them by the balls, the hearts and minds generally follow."

Machiavelli saw at first hand the ruin of an unarmed prophet: Girolamo Savonarola, a Benedictine priest of fiery moralism whose severe piety inspired the Florentines in the last decade of the sixteenth century to an extraordinary and quite atypical religious austerity. Mothers dispatched their wet-nurses and fed their babies from their own breasts; costumes and masks for carnival were considered vanities and, along with impious books and works of art, were consigned to the bonfires. Papal and aristocratic excesses were denounced and were presented as evidence of the imminent end of the material world and the arrival of the End of Days. It was widely believed that Savonarola conversed with God. In 1498, just as Machiavelli was about to start his service to the republic, the Florentines revolted, and Savonarola was broken on the rack and then burned to death in the Piazza della Signoria, where a simple bronze plaque still marks the location of the stake.

Machiavelli's favorite example of the armed prophet and his greatest hero is Moses. At God's behest, Moses leads the

Israelites out of Egypt and across the desert toward the Promised Land. He leaves them briefly to climb Mount Sinai, where he receives God's sacred commandments. Descending the mountain, he sees with horror the idolatrous orgy around the golden calf. He smashes the tablets and asks Aaron, his brother, for an explanation, to which Aaron replies, "Let not thy anger wax hot; thou knowest the people, that they are set on evil." We are by now familiar with this notion. Then comes the part that most people have forgotten, or never knew, but which Machiavelli knows well and appreciates:

> Then Moses stood in the gate of the camp, and said: "Whoso is on the Lord's side, let him come unto me." And all the sons of Levi gathered themselves together unto him. And he said unto them: "Thus saith the Lord, the God of Israel: Put ye every man his sword upon his thigh, and go to and fro from gate to gate throughout the camp, and slay every man his brother, and every man his companion, and every man his neighbor." And the sons of Levi did according to the word of Moses; and there fell of the people that day about three thousand men.[3]

Machiavelli notes, "Whoever reads the Bible sensibly will see that Moses was forced, were his laws and institutions to go forward, to kill numberless men."[4] No hypocrisy here (just overstatement); Machiavelli doesn't pretend that the means used by Moses were good. He knows that somewhere in the shards of the shattered tablets it says "Thou shalt not murder." He readily admits that the means are evil, but he insists that they are the only ones that work *in such dire circumstances*. If Moses had said to the idolaters "Let us reason together," he would have failed. In these circumstances, to do good—is to guarantee the triumph of evil. Machiavelli expands the earlier paradox: just as the quest for peace at any price invites war and, worse than war, defeat and domination, so good acts sometimes advance the triumph of evil, as there are circumstances when only doing evil ensures the victory of a good cause.

ENTERING INTO EVIL

Machiavelli is commonly taken to be saying that the ends always justify the means, but he does not believe that. Quite the contrary. He simply recognizes the reality that there are times when a leader must accept dreadful responsibility in serving the common good.

We all know this to be true. Consider the story of Henry Tandey, a British infantryman in the Duke of Wellington Regiment in the First World War. On September 28, 1918, Tandey participated in an attack against enemy trenches near the small French town of Marcoing. The British carried the day, and as they advanced, Tandey cautiously peered into a trench. He saw an enemy soldier, a corporal, lying bleeding on the ground. It would have been easy for Tandey to finish off his enemy, as he had killed many that day; Tandey had played an heroic role in the battle and later was awarded the Victoria Cross, the highest wartime decoration, for his great courage. But he felt it was wrong to shoot an injured man, and he spared the corporal's life.

In 1940, during the Nazi bombardment of Coventry, where Tandey worked as a security guard at the Triumph automobile factory, he gnashed his teeth. "Had I known what that corporal was going to become! God knows how sad I am that I spared him." The corporal was Adolf Hitler. Tandey's humane gesture had led to the deaths of millions of people and, in a bitter irony of military destiny, had placed his own life at the mercy of the monster whose life he could have taken.

Murder is surely evil, yet every reasonable person will agree that the cause of good would have been greatly advanced if Henry Tandey had killed Hitler in that trench. History abounds with examples of good actions furthering the cause of evil. When Jimmy Carter was president, he was so appalled by the assassinations that had been carried out by American officers and agents that he issued a stern executive order forbidding the practice. This had the unanticipated consequence of favoring the forces of evil, because we could not go after individual terrorists. We could either ask foreign governments to arrest the terrorists for us (not bloody likely!) or take massive action against a larger target (like a terrorist military base or training facility), thereby greatly increasing the odds of killing innocent civilians. In his moralistic attempt to make murder less likely, Carter made it *more* likely, by both our enemies and ourselves.

Lying is evil, yet the success of the Normandy landing—D-Day—during the Second World War was greatly aided by feeding false information to the Nazis, so that they expected an invasion at a different time and in a different place. Not a mere white lie, this was an enormous deception, with a magnificent result. Lying is essential to the survival of nations and to the success of great enterprises, because if your enemies can count on the reliability of everything you say, your vulnerability is enormously increased. Like all successful enterprises, nations practice strategic deception on one another, camouflaging their weapons, hiding their plans, even lying to allies or their own people to ensure continued loyalty and maintain morale.

All's fair in war . . . and in love. Practicing deceit to fulfill your heart's desire might be not only legitimate, but delicious! In one of his lighter moments Machiavelli hails it in verse.

So suave is deceit
brought to its imagined and dear purpose
that divests another of effort
and makes every bitter taste sweet.
O remedy high and rare,
you show the straight path to erring souls,
you with your great valor,
in making another blessed, make Love rich:
You conquer, with your saintly counsels,
stones, poisons, and charms.[5]

Deceit is rarely so amusing and gratifying. Sometimes you may even have to sacrifice your own people to sustain a necessary deception. The British broke the most secret Nazi military code, and learned that the Germans were planning to bomb the city of Coventry. Had Churchill acted to save the lives of the city's inhabitants, the Germans could have deduced that their communications were not secure, and might have changed the code. Churchill accordingly took no special steps to protect the residents of Coventry, concealing the truth about the state of his knowledge from Hitler's generals at the cost of British lives. Churchill understood that great commanders must have an "element of legerdemain, an original and sinister touch, which leaves the enemy puzzled as well as beaten."[6]

The Soviets were masters at sacrificing the lives of their

own people to create or enhance a strategic deception. Shortly after the revolution, the Bolsheviks actually created a phony anti-Soviet organization in the West in order to lure the real anti-Communists inside. To establish the bona fides of their organization—known as "the Trust"—they arranged for successful sabotage and even assassination to be carried out against targets inside the Soviet Union. The French and British were impressed, especially since they themselves had been singularly unsuccessful at getting their agents into key positions within Lenin's dictatorship, and they financed the Trust. Worse still, they put key Trust leaders in touch with genuine anti-Soviet organizations. This enabled the Kremlin not only to learn the intentions of their enemies but also to manipulate the anti-Communists and eventually to destroy them (one of their victims was the celebrated British adventurer, "Reilly, ace of spies"), thus exceeding Lenin's prediction that the capitalists would provide the rope he would use to hang them. In this case, they even paid for the rope.

The *Soldier's Pocket Book,* written in the late nineteenth century, contained sound Machiavellian advice from its author, the British general Viscount Garnet Wolseley: "We will keep hammering along with the conviction that honesty is the best policy, and that truth always wins in the long run. These pretty little sentiments do well for a child's copy book, but a man who acts on them had better sheathe his sword forever."[7]

Here is the crux of the moral issue. Machiavelli agrees with those who say that only extreme situations justify extreme measures like killing and lying, but with one very big caveat: if the situation requires it, you've got to do what works. This leads to what De Grazia has aptly termed Machiavelli's un-golden rule: "Do unto others as they would do unto you." If you're dealing with honorable people, you must be honorable yourself, but if you're fighting implacable enemies, you must not be bound by rules they are preparing to trample on. As Churchill acidly remarked during the Second World War, it would have been folly for the Western leaders to weaken themselves by strictly observing the letter of the law, while the Nazis and fascists were trying to destroy civilized society and impose a racist dictatorship.

Machiavelli knows that it is a terrible anguish for a good man to perform evil acts, even to accomplish an honorable result, and he tries to ease the anguish by assuring leaders that if they act effectively their contact with evil will be temporary. If you do it well, you will not be eternally tarnished. He chooses his words carefully: "enter into evil." Once the dirty deed is done, you can exit. Indeed, you *must* exit.

This is the basic test for a leader facing the awful choice of entering into evil or sticking to the straight and narrow: Will he make things better or worse? It is wrong to behave ethically if by so doing you open the door to enemies who will destroy all possibility of an ethical world, or open the floodgates to those who would destroy you. It is also wrong to abjure evil acts if your inaction produces even more evil. Consider the spectacular case of Turkey in the late 1970s, when that nation was inundated by a terrorist wave without precedent. It was estimated that, at the peak of the madness, one person died at the hands of terrorists every ten minutes or so. The feeble multiparty democracy—nine minority governments had briefly held office in seven years—couldn't deal with it, and the military seized power in the fall of 1980. In the next two years, 43,000 persons were arrested on charges of terrorism, and 734,000 weapons were confiscated. Turkey was denounced for its insensitive repression and violation of human rights; with the 1978 hit movie *Midnight Express,* the country became the symbol of hateful military dictatorship.

Machiavelli would say that the evil actions were caused by the unworthy leaders who permitted the situation to get out of hand. Had they acted firmly against the terrorists before murder had become the daily fare of Turkish citizens, tens of thousands of innocent lives would have been saved, democracy would have endured, and the evil actions of the military junta would not have been necessary.

A prince must not worry about the reproach of cruelty when it is a matter of keeping his subjects united and loyal; for with a very few examples of cruelty he will be more compassionate than those who, out of excessive mercy, permit disorders to continue, from which arise murders and plundering; for these usually harm the community at large, while the executions that come from the prince harm particular individuals."[8]

Machiavelli would approve the actions of the Turkish army, for their drastic discipline worked. Not only was terrorism wiped out, but the army supervised free elections at the end of 1983 and then stepped aside, turning the country over to Turgut Ozal, who became one of the country's greatest leaders.

The Turkish military fulfilled Machiavelli's other requirement for entering into evil: the evil actions must be limited to meeting a specific crisis and must not become an integral part of the government or regime. Each time the Turkish armed forces felt obliged to intervene they did so for a brief period, and they were at pains to keep their word to the nation by leaving power once the crisis had been overcome. The Turkish military leaders are not to be confused with most African presidents, who view themselves as leaders for life, or the heads of the old military dictatorships in Latin America. Such tyrants would never dream of emulating the Turkish generals by insisting that the political class fulfill its obligations and govern the nation.

Machiavelli would despise the institutionalized terror of

the modern totalitarian state. Indeed, he reserves some of his harshest language for those leaders who create tyrannies: "Vile and detestable are those who destroy religion, shatter monarchies and republics, those enemies of virtue, letters and all other arts that bring honor and utility to mankind."[9] Machiavelli wants virtuous leaders who create great enterprises, not usurpers of power who dominate others for their own pleasure. He denounces the cruel tyrant Agathocles of ancient Syracuse, who ruled from 317 B.C. until his death in 289 B.C. Agathocles achieved "imperium, not glory," Machiavelli says, because "it cannot be called virtue to kill one's own citizens, betray friends, be without faith, without mercy, without religion."[10] Agathocles was a winner: he conquered the city with his army, banished or murdered some ten thousand citizens to consolidate his rule, and extended his power to the point where he could proclaim himself king of all Sicily. Moreover, he greatly enriched the state and caused many elegant public buildings to be constructed. Yet Machiavelli denounces him because Agathocles destroyed the republic of Syracuse and maintained his personal tyranny by the continuous use of evil measures. He did not exit from evil, thereby becoming an "enemy of virtue."

There are several circumstances in which good leaders are likely to have to enter into evil: whenever the very existence of the nation is threatened; when the state is first created or revolutionary change is to be accomplished; when removing an evil tyrant; and when the society becomes corrupt and must be restored to virtue. We've already looked at the first (war), and tyrannicide speaks for itself. Saving a state that has sunk into corruption is Machiavelli's most passionate concern—it is why he wrote *The Prince*—and will be the subject of the last chapter of this book. Revolution warrants an immediate look.

REVOLUTION

Look at the map of the world: national boundaries have not been drawn by peaceful men leading lives of spiritual con-templation. National borders have been established by war, and national character has been shaped by struggle, most of-ten bloody struggle. "States are not held with paternosters in hand," as Cosimo de' Medici once remarked. Moses created a new state and a new religion, which makes him one of the most revolutionary leaders of all time. His revolution could not have succeeded if, as he himself wished, he had led by ex-ample alone. Moses led the Israelites out of bondage, guided them through the wilderness by divine light, and nourished them with manna falling from heaven. To no avail! No sooner had he left them to their own devices, they demanded new gods to worship. The execution of the sinners was necessary to confirm Moses' authority. His appeal to their hearts and minds wasn't sufficient. Machiavelli might have used the example of Mohammed, who also founded a state and a religion. The founder of Islam understood equally well what had to be done, and backed up his religious vision with the force of arms.

All serious revolutionaries realize that power must be effectively, and sometimes ruthlessly, exercised if the revolution is to succeed, because revolution invariably attracts more opponents than supporters. Changing the very nature of the state, Machiavelli warns us, is the most dangerous of political undertakings, and the least likely to prevail, because everyone who benefited from the old order will be against you and will fight to recover past privileges. Those who stand to gain as a result of your actions will initially be merely halfhearted supporters, because men "have no faith in new things until they see issue from them a firm result."[11] They will become believers and supporters only if they see that you are effective. We are back to François Mitterrand and Vince Lombardi: winning is everything.

During his ill-fated campaign to change the American health-care system in the first two years of his presidency, Bill Clinton repeatedly quoted Machiavelli's observations on revolution in order to explain the difficulty of his own efforts and the intensity of the opposition. But Clinton missed the point:

health-care reform does not a revolution make. Machiavelli is talking about a change in the basic order of the state, a fundamental revolution. As for reform of the sort Clinton was advocating, Machiavelli recognizes that most people welcome innovation, and will rally around leaders who appear to be bold. By Machiavelli's lights, Clinton had all the advantages, at least going in. The more appropriate observation from Machiavelli was one Clinton was not inclined to quote: "Let princes not complain of the faults committed by the people subjected to their authority, for they result entirely from their own negligence or bad example."[12]

Nothing is more pathetic than so-called revolutionaries who shrink from the requirements of their task. The Russian Revolution was launched by Alexandr Kerensky, a decent and reasonable man who prided himself on maintaining high ethical standards. Kerensky replaced the Czar but was no match for the ruthless Bolsheviks, who took revolution more seriously.

Lenin treated politics as warfare. . . . The others did not take this dictum quite as literally as did Lenin. Whereas they thought of it as ordinary conflict, he and he alone saw its purpose as conquering power and annihilating all rivals. By annihilation, he meant, not merely eliminating them as competitors, but physically exterminating them.[13]

Lenin also extirpated the entire royal family, in keeping with Machiavelli's dictum that when you take over a state governed by a single ruler or a single family, you must wipe out the entire line, so no one will be left to claim the legitimacy of the fallen regime. If some are left alive, there is a grave risk that they will rally the people against you and regain power. After the French Revolution had run its course, the Bourbon monarchy was restored. The Leninists in Russia ran no such risk, for no Romanovs survived.

The same general principle applies to the Western democracies, but our political killing is mostly symbolic (although countries like Italy routinely experience political assassination, and American presidents are sometimes targeted). States governed by a political party—the democratic equivalent of a ruling family—undergo the same kind of purge following elections. If the party in power is defeated, the new governing party removes the old guard and installs its own people in positions of power. In the United States, a new president purges thousands of "political appointees" from the previous administration and replaces them with his followers. Not only cabinet secretaries, but undersecretaries, assistant secretaries, deputy assistant secretaries and even, under Clinton, the staff of the White House Travel Office, whom he purged, and all U.S. attorneys general, whom he fired en bloc as soon as he took office, fall under political control. All serve "at the pleasure of the president." The old "royal family" is (politically) obliterated. And so it is in business, where a new CEO has enormous latitude in selecting his staff, as well as in sports, where a new coach generally brings his own assistants and frequently makes drastic changes in the team itself. As Leo Durocher, a tough-minded and very successful leader of men on the baseball field, bluntly commented, "Nice guys finish last."

Machiavelli is not telling you to *be* evil, he is simply stating the facts: if you lead, there will be occasions when you will have to do unpleasant, even evil, things or be destroyed. If you are lucky, these occasions will be few and far between; a leader who never had to do such things would be fortunate indeed. For the rest, he wants you to be and do good, convinced as he is that the proper mission of great leaders is to achieve the *common* good, to fashion good laws and enforce them with good arms and good religion. He wants you to achieve glory and goodness for all your people, and thus for yourself. Only such an accomplishment is worth the energies and passions of great men and women.

THE GOOD SOCIETY

Obviously, this imperative to strive for the common good does not come from human instinct; our instincts are not nearly so

noble. The goal of achieving the common good comes from
the highest authority: God himself. The act "most gratifying
to God" is one that benefits one's country, and Machiavelli is
quite outspoken about the best form of government. Notwith-
standing his infamy as the tutor of dictators, he favors republics, and does so for reasons we can now understand: a
single ruler is more likely to be corrupted by wealth and
power than the people, who will have less of each, and the
single ruler will be more likely to advance his own interests
than those of the whole state. There have been great single
leaders, and there are times and places when only a single
leader can lead the people to greatness, but it is a risky enterprise, because the worst government is tyranny. Machiavelli
openly calls for the overthrow of tyrants, and devotes the
longest chapter of the *Discourses* to explaining the organization of a successful conspiracy.

He has contempt for those who slander the people, because
he believes the people are likely to make better decisions than
a single ruler. "This common good," he writes in the *Discourses,* "is observed nowhere but in a republic. . . . It is no
wonder then that ancient peoples persecuted tyrants with so
much hate and loved the free way of life." He goes further
still: while the creation of a good state depends on one great
leader or a handful of great leaders, "The people are superior
in maintaining those institutions, laws, and ordinances, which

certainly places them on a par with those who established them."[14] This in a chapter entitled bluntly "The People Are Wiser Than Princes." Indeed, in a republic, "The people are the princes." And he praises free enterprise, private property, and minimal taxation:

> All lands and all countries that are in all respects free . . . derive greatest profit. For there one sees greater populations, because of marriages being freer, and more desired by men: because each one procreates willingly those children he thinks he can nourish, not worrying that [his] patrimony may be taken from him, and that one knows not only that they are born free and not slaves, but they through their virtue may become princes. Riches multiply there in greater number."[15]

The best state is a meritocracy ("children . . . through their virtue may become princes"), in which as many people as possible have maximum freedom and power, for "it is not without good reason that it is said 'The voice of the people is the voice of God.'" Moreover, there is less danger to the common good from the people than from a bad leader, for a single leader is often "misled by his own passions, which are far greater than those of the people." And the people's errors are more easily corrected than those of the ruler:

A licentious and mutinous people may easily be brought back to good conduct by the influence and persuasion of a good man, but an evil-minded prince is not amenable to such influences, and therefore there is no other remedy against him but cold steel.[16]

Machiavelli's notion of the good state calls to mind *The Federalist Papers* when he writes: "When there is combined under the same constitution a prince, a nobility, and the power of the people, then these three powers will watch and keep each other reciprocally in check."[17] This anticipates Madison and Hamilton (who knew his works), and he is certainly aware that Sparta, which had a mixed constitution, lasted eight hundred years, a record.

In fact, there is much in Machiavelli that sounds like the American Founding Fathers, as there is much that sounds like the puritanism of the early colonies. Like the men who wrote the Constitution, he is a great believer in the rule of law. "Whoever is not controlled by laws will commit the same errors as an unbridled multitude,"[18] he insists as sternly as Hamilton or Franklin. Like the Puritans, he despises sloth and self-indulgence and dreads the corrupting force of wealth. He believes that hard work helps make men virtuous, and, although not a regular churchgoer himself, he knows that a good state must rest on a religious foundation. To remain good, a state must "above every other thing keep the ceremonies of their religion incorrupt and keep them always in their veneration, because one can have no greater indicator of the wreck of a land than to see the divine cult scorned."[19]

He rails against the propertied classes, the rich and lazy who live in luxury off the income of their inherited lands instead of creating new wealth through hard work and enterprise. Machiavelli's motto for a successful republican society is "Poor citizens, rich state." The wealth created by the most successful citizens should be put to the common good. This, too, is part of a long-standing American tradition, even among the very wealthy. "A man who dies rich . . . dies disgraced," the millionaire philanthropist Andrew Carnegie wrote, and he warned that giving wealth to a child drained him of ambition and subverted his character. Each generation should be made to demonstrate its worth through its own efforts.

Machiavelli fears the conflicts that derive from the radically unequal distribution of wealth, not because he expects the poor, driven by envy, to rise up against the rich, but because he knows that the rich—as distinct from the slothful landowners—will never be satisfied with what they have and will constantly seek more. And because the rich have a great capacity to disrupt society in their quest for even more, they will often exceed the boundaries of acceptable action. It is this "impermissible and ambitious behavior" that drives the poor to revolt, both to "avenge themselves against [the rich] by despoiling them, or in order to enable them to have access to those riches and honors they see badly used." If the rich were content with their wealth, and did not want more, and behaved virtuously by working for the common good, the unequal distribution of wealth would not be so socially and politically explosive. But they cannot behave this way; they will never cease their efforts to aggrandize. He concludes that there must be a fairly egalitarian distribution of wealth for a republic to succeed, whereas in a society with deep class divisions, government by an elite or a single ruler is more likely to endure.

The greatest obstacle to the creation and survival of a good state is man himself. As we always seek more, we will be reluctant to put our riches at the service of others, let alone of the common good. We will only do this if compelled, or inspired. This is the task of government. Machiavelli prefers republics, but good government can be achieved by single rulers and oligarchies as well, provided the leaders are good and they understand how to rule effectively. The winning formula is threefold: good laws, good arms, good religion. We are back to Moses.

CHAPTER FIVE

HOW TO RULE

> You know that the chief duty of every prince is to keep
> himself from being hated and despised. . . . whenever he
> does that well, everything must go well.

Any state, any organization, even the freest and most democratic, requires strong leadership, because only such leaders
can restrain the ruinous impulses that drive human actions,
and force men to act for the common good. We must *not* be
left to our own ruinous devices, but instead must be made to
do the right thing. "Men work nothing well if not through necessity; but where choice abounds, and where one can become
licentious, everything immediately fills up with confusion and
disorder."[1]

The usual Machiavellian paradox: compulsion—or necessity, as he terms it—makes men noble, and enables them to remain free, while abundant choice is dangerous, leads to chaos,

and leaves men at the mercy of their enemies. The generals, the businessmen, and the athletic coaches know this, but political leaders and journalists often forget it. They get carried away by demands for absolute freedom, forgetting that freedom produces anarchy unless tempered by the well-defined sense of responsibility that comes from good laws and good religion. It is not the "free spirit" who shows the greatest courage, but rather the disciplined fighter who learns to overcome his fears and risks his life for the common good. As General George Patton, whose exploits in the Second World War made him one of the great American military commanders, put it:

> All human beings have an innate resistance to obedience. Discipline removes this resistance and, by constant repetition, makes obedience habitual and subconscious. . . . No sane man is unafraid in battle, but discipline produces in him a form of vicarious courage which, with his manhood, makes for victory.[2]

Discipline is also required to restrain mass hysteria. The people are easily manipulated by demagogues, and the voice of reason is easily overwhelmed by collective rage or passion, even when the survival of the nation is at stake. Even contemporary Europeans and Canadians, who should have learned that ethnic nationalism often leads to catastrophe, are beset with separatist movements led by charismatic figures. From the Spanish Basques and the Belgian Walloons to Serbs, Croats, and Bosnians to Canadian Québecois, northern Italians, and the Northern Irish, great masses of people are driven by cries for revenge for ancient offenses, real or imagined.

The greatest example of the sort of destructive hysteria Machiavelli has in mind is modern terrorism. The spectacular story of the Uruguayan Tupamaros in the 1960s illustrates the phenomenon Machiavelli writes about in a chapter of the *Discourses* entitled "The People Often Seeks Its Own Ruin . . ." The contemporary historian Walter Laqueur describes the Uruguayan terrorists:

> They did not, on the whole, engage in indiscriminate murder, they wept when they killed (but they killed). They were genuine idealists. . . . Their activities were initially quite successful, proving that civilian government could easily be disrupted and providing striking headlines for the world press. But, in the final analysis, the only result of their campaign was the destruction of freedom in a country which, alone in Latin America, had an unbroken democratic tradition of many decades and which had been the first Latin American welfare state. . . . The Tupamaros' campaign resulted in the emergence of a right-wing military dictatorship; in de-

stroying the democratic system, they also destroyed their own movement.[3]

It was twenty years before Uruguay returned to democracy.

The tools of discipline—arms, laws, and religion—are common to all well-constituted states, and if any of the three is lacking or enfeebled, the survival of the state is mortally threatened. The leader's primary task is therefore to maintain these three crucial elements of statecraft, and periodically to renew, refresh, and reinvigorate them. All three compel men to repress their dangerous instincts and act virtuously. This is accomplished by fear. Without fear of God no state can last long, for the dread of eternal damnation keeps men in line, causes them to honor their promises, and inspires them to risk their lives for the common good: "How can those who scorn God revere men?"[4] Without fear of punishment, men will not obey laws that force them to act contrary to their passions. Without fear of arms, the state cannot enforce the laws, or defend itself from its enemies.

To this end, Machiavelli wants leaders to make the state spectacular. Rewards and punishments should make a forceful impression on the citizens. Machiavelli insists that no mercy should be shown in enforcing the law, even to those who have earned the gratitude of the nation for past acts. Moreover, the law should not be merely enforced, it should be given grandeur. Punishment, including executions, should be public, so that the fearful effect is magnified. Religion should not be merely observed, it should be celebrated. If possible, laws and religion should be brought to life by heroes, whose behavior is "of such reputation and of such example that good men desire to imitate and the bad are ashamed to lead a life contrary to them."[5] If the stagecraft is successful, the leader will have less trouble maintaining order.

To be sure, not all laws and religions are good. In particular, the Christianity Machiavelli sees at work around him—the same Roman Catholic church that would shortly drive Martin Luther into open opposition—has corrupted the heroic ideal. Christianity "glorifies more the humble and contemplative [men] than the men of action," and it constantly diverts our attention and energies from the earthly tasks at hand. Christianity praises humility and disdains "the honor of the world," while the more virile religions of antiquity "only blessed men full of earthly glory." By focusing our eyes on heaven and making us "more disposed to endure injuries than to avenge them," he laments, we are turned into easy prey for evil enemies. The triumph of virtue is postponed to another life, beyond the here and now, and men are urged to accept their fate, no matter how great their misery. Even defeat and domination can be endured, because the ultimate victory awaits in the afterlife.

Machiavelli insists that this is a tragic misunderstanding,

and the history of Christianity certainly provides abundant examples of more aggressive readings of the New Testament. He blames the error on "the baseness of men who have interpreted our religion according to the promptings of indolence rather than those of virtue." His own reading is quite different. Since Christianity permits us to defend our country, it follows that defense of the nation is a high calling indeed. Machiavelli is intensely patriotic, and he has no doubt that God approves. "I believe," he fervently pronounces, "that the greatest good that one can do, and the most gratifying to God, is that which one does for one's country."[6] Since it is the highest good, the defense of the country is one of those extreme situations in which a leader is justified in committing evil. If one's country is threatened, Machiavelli insists, "there should fall no consideration whatever of either just or unjust, kind or cruel, praiseworthy or ignominious."[7] But you can't defend your country with priests and martyrs armed only with their prayers and incantations, and thus the kind of Christianity Machiavelli seeks will revive ancient traditions, which held that the supreme good was to be found in "greatness of spirit, strength of body, and all those qualities that render men formidable."[8] Nations led by such men are difficult to dominate.

Good religion teaches men that politics is the most important enterprise in the eyes of God. Like Moses, Machiavelli wants the law of his state to be seen, and therefore obeyed, as divinely ordered. The combination of fear of God and fear of punishment—duly carried out with good arms—provides the necessary discipline for good government. The extreme case is war, when men are called upon to sacrifice, if need be to die, for the good of the state. Dying for one's country doesn't come naturally. Modern armies, raised from the populace, must be inspired, motivated, indoctrinated. Religion is central to the military enterprise, for men are more likely to risk their lives if they believe they will be rewarded forever after for serving their country, while they will be doomed to hellfire for eternity if they betray the nation. The great seventeenth-century Swedish king and military commander, Gustavus Adolphus, put this principle to work:

> Gustavus fully understood the binding and driving force of religion. . . . [He] introduced regular morning and evening prayers, and distributed through the army a special soldiers' Prayer-Book, and the common sight of generals and privates kneeling side by side in prayer left an indelible impression. . . . In the "Articles of War," which he wrote in his own hand . . . among the offences punishable by death were pillage, violence to women, and . . . "despising divine service, third offence."[9]

Fear enhances discipline, as does affection. The people must fear their leaders, but they must also believe in the goodness of their leaders. The operative word here is 'Machiavelli knows you will not always *be* good, but you must usually try to *be seen as* good. The first principle of good statecraft is to win popular support, and although it is particularly important in a republic—"Without satisfying the generality of men, one never made a stable republic"—this rule applies to all forms of leadership. Indeed, even in *The Prince,* which was written at a time of terrible crisis, when Machiavelli believed that only a dictator could rescue his country (and therefore was entitled to enter into evil), he devotes considerable space to the qualities a single ruler should have, or at least appear to have: humaneness, compassion, religious faith and truthfulness. Machiavelli is the first image maker. He knows that brute force is not enough; the people must also be entranced.

Machiavelli describes this double requirement of power and charm, courage and cunning, by saying that leaders must imitate the qualities of both the lion and the fox. The fox is clever and charming, but is not strong enough to defend himself, while the lion can win any fight, but isn't smart enough to avoid traps set by his enemies. To follow one as a model to the exclusion of the other would be fatal.

No contemporary leader would find anything unusual about being told to attend constantly to his image. We know how fickle people are. Ingratitude, Machiavelli ruefully observes in a poem, is the daughter of Greed and Suspicion, nursed in the arms of Envy, and has been an essential part of human nature ever since Adam and Eve ungratefully ate the apple and departed Eden. The people will not remember your past services; you must remain alert to shifts in their mood.

This does not mean, however, that Machiavelli approves the sort of contemporary politician who reads the public opinion polls every day and conducts himself accordingly. Modern politics are so concerned with image that at times one wonders if there is any serious intent, or simply an unending campaign of image enhancement. The people may eventually see such behavior as a sign of weakness, and become contemptuous, which is likely to be fatal.

There is another reason to avoid rule by public opinion poll that is in keeping with Machiavelli's understanding of human nature; the qualities the people *say* they esteem in a leader are not necessarily those that they will actually appreciate. For example, take the quality of generosity. Is it better for a leader to be considered generous or miserly? Is it better to have a government that bends over backward to tend to the material needs and desires of the populace, or one that tightfistedly doles out wealth from the treasury? The answer is: it all depends. If you are consistently miserly, the people may grumble, but it isn't serious enough to cost you your position. If you base your reputation on generosity, you will fall prey to the insatiability of human desire. Once the people decide you are generous, you will be called upon to be increasingly munificent, and sooner or later you will run out of money. You will then have either to raise taxes in order to maintain the level of spending, or give less to the people. This runs the greatest of all risks for a leader: the people will hate you, either for taking their wealth, or for becoming a miser. Better to be miserly in the first place; it doesn't risk your authority.

The politicians currently struggling to reform the modern welfare state can testify to the brilliance of Machiavelli's analysis, for they are now being battered between the rock of ruinously generous spending (lengthy vacations, generous salaries, universal health care, child care, maternity leave, and munificent pensions), and the hard place of increasingly hated taxes. Their survival in office is threatened no matter which way they turn. A strong leader would explain the real situation, announce that the fat years are over, at least for a time, and promise to share the burdens equitably among all the people. The good leader would pay the political price at once, both because he knows that the policy is in the best interests of the state, and because—if he can convince the people to stay the course—he will later be able to take credit for saving the national economy and restoring virtue to public finance. Machiavelli remarks that just as evil actions should be taken in a single stroke, merely unpopular steps should also be done quickly, rather than being dragged out over time. Measures to avoid war at all costs invite worse consequences, and efforts to mitigate pain from public policy more often than not lead to even greater pain for more and more people.

Machiavelli insists that leaders look at the political consequences of their actions, rather than pondering the questions abstractly. Keep your eye on the ball! You're going to have to decree unpopular actions, but you'll have the chance to do some very popular things as well. Don't be deceived by the instant reaction of the people in either case, because on close examination a wise leader will realize that "something which appears to be a virtue, if pursued, will end in his destruction; while some other thing which seems to be a vice, if pursued, will result in his safety and his well-being."[10] Things are rarely what they seem to be, and you should not be deceived by appearances; you must sometimes, however, use appearances—above all your own—to convince others that you are what they want you to be, even when you're not.

IS IT BETTER TO BE LOVED OR FEARED?

In one of his most celebrated passages, Machiavelli poses the essential question about the relationship between leaders and followers: Is it more effective to enforce discipline by rigorously applying the laws, and unhesitatingly exercising your power (making you more feared than loved), or by winning the affection of your followers by the force of your virtuous example (making you more loved than feared)? He hastens to say that it would be best to be both loved and feared, choosing the one style or the other according to circumstances. Leaders should use both carrots and sticks, giving rewards when they have been earned, and punishing malefactors when necessary. But walking such a narrow tightrope is asking too much; "Our nature does not permit it."[11] Unless you're very lucky—unless you inherit a well-organized enterprise with good people— you'll have to choose.

You must have the support of the people, but they are fickle, and will turn on you the moment you fail. To base your rule solely, or primarily, on the people's affection for you is as risky as constructing your image on generosity, and for precisely the same reason. If you prosper and win, they will hail you; but if you lose, they'll turn on you. Which is the safer method?

You can certainly lead effectively by earning the affection of the people. Machiavelli knows that even a military commander can rule by the force of his virtuous example; affection can be as powerful as fear. No less an authority than Plutarch wrote that "the greatest talent of a general is to secure obedience through the affection he inspires." American history is replete with examples of this principle, beginning with George Washington. During the latter stages of the Revolutionary War, some American soldiers were enraged by the constant delay in the arrival of their wages, and the apparent lack of esteem from the Continental Congress. In Newburgh, New York, Washington addressed the troops in an attempt to calm them. In one of his most moving speeches, he implored the men to ignore calls for mass protest, hoping that "you will, by the dignity of your conduct, afford occasion for posterity to say, when speaking of the glorious example you have exhibited to mankind, 'Had this day been wanting, the world had never seen the last stage of perfection to which human nature is capable of attaining.'" He then began to read a letter from a member of Congress, but the handwriting was very difficult to make out. Washington, a vain man, had not used spectacles in public, but there was no alternative. As he awkwardly put his glasses on, he ruefully said to the men, "Gentlemen, you must pardon me. I have grown gray in your service and now find myself growing blind."[12] He carried the day, and the story of Newburgh became an important chapter in the life story of the "Father of his Country."

It works—Robert E. Lee had a similar relationship with his soldiers—and it certainly feels better than giving your people tough-love. Who wouldn't rather be loved than feared? But there are problems. The main problem is that it makes you *personally* the focus, even the symbol, of rule. If you seek constantly to endear yourself to the people, and make yourself the symbol of the nation or the company, you will be unable to avoid popular wrath when things go wrong, as Moses discovered in the wilderness at the foot of Mount Sinai. The leader who rigidly applies the laws, on the other hand, is protected from popular hatred because he is simply "going by the book." If the people are unhappy, their complaint will be primarily with the laws; it's not your fault. You don't want to be seen as the person responsible for all the actions of the enterprise. You want to get credit for the good news, but you want others blamed for the bad.

The second problem is that ruling by love takes the initiative out of your hands and leaves it to others. "Men love at their own pleasure and fear at the pleasure of the prince," Machiavelli reminds us, and we know how dangerous *that* is. Even if you are a master of manipulation of public opinion, and even if you have achieved glory beyond all dreaming, you may still be ruined by ingratitude and envy. It is more prudent to assert your power, making it clear that those who cross you will regret it:

Men have less scruple in offending one who makes himself loved than one who makes himself feared; for love is held by a chain of obligation which, men being selfish, is broken whenever it serves their purpose; but fear is maintained by a dread of punishment which never fails.[13]

To be an effective leader, the most prudent method is to ensure that your people are afraid of you. To instill that fear, you must demonstrate that those who attack you will not survive. George Washington was well aware of the importance of decisive action against those who challenged his authority. In his first term as president, he faced the 1794 Whisky Insurrection, of citizens refusing to pay excise taxes on their liquor manufactures. His report to the Congress echoes the urgency of Machiavelli's advice: "A prejudice, fostered and embittered by the artifice of men who labored for an ascendancy over the will of others by the guidance of their passions, produced symptoms of riot and violence." Washington sadly observed that efforts to deal reasonably with the taxpayers' complaints only made things worse: "The very forbearance to press prosecutions was misinterpreted into a fear of urging the execution of the laws; and associations of men began to denounce threats against the officers employed."[14] Washington called out the army and personally led it against the insurrection. No American president was ever so loved as George Washington, but he knew that fear was essential to his effective rule.

No contemporary leader has mastered the skills of rule more effectively than Yasser Arafat, who has managed to be both loved and feared and has brilliantly used deception to create different images of himself for friends and enemies. Arafat had to kill potential challengers to retain control of the

P.L.O. yet it was also important for him to appear to be a "moderate" in order to be accepted as a legitimate player in the Middle East "peace process." He therefore had his intelligence services secretly create the Abu Nidal terrorist organization, which Arafat used to assassinate his enemies within the Palestinian movement. At the same time, the existence of such a violent and murderous group enabled Arafat to successfully pose as a "moderate." The assassinations were blamed solely on Abu Nidal, while Arafat maintained a lofty pose and spoke of peace. The deception succeeded fully. Even the Israelis were unaware of Arafat's strategy, until Ion Mihai Pacepa, the head of the Romanian intelligence service, defected to the United States in the late 1970s and revealed the scheme.

Arafat spoke of peace in English to foreign diplomats, and promised his own people in Arabic that Israel would eventually be destroyed. His considerable diplomatic accomplishments always took place against a background of violence; Israel's leaders signed a peace agreement with him after Arafat unleashed a bloody intifada against Israel. Throughout the "peace process," his reputation as a moderate and a man of peace grew apace with the increasing tempo of the killing of Israelis by Palestinians whom he publicly praised and embraced. He was even rewarded with a share of the Nobel Peace Prize, an irony Machiavelli would have appreciated. Arafat's great success is a monument to the wisdom of Machiavelli's advice that it is much safer for a leader to be feared than loved. Indeed, if you are feared, your followers will always find reasons to love you.

The current array of Western leaders have usually gotten this one hopelessly wrong, while the great leaders of the previous generation understood it, and changed the world. From the mid-seventies to the late eighties, the West was blessed with a remarkable number of men and women who fought bravely for their countries and for their own glory:

- King Juan Carlos of Spain defied the "experts" who predicted that Spain would disintegrate into civil war after the death of the dictator Francisco Franco. Instead, he used the authority of the crown and his own personal courage to lead his nation to becoming a successful democracy. This established a model that was copied all over the world, first in Latin America, then in Poland, and even in South Africa. See Michael A. Ledeen, *Freedom Betrayed* (Washington, 1996) pp. 15ff.

- Pope John Paul II used his own personal bravery, and, just as Machiavelli had hoped, the power of religious faith to mobilize millions of people in a struggle against tyranny. While constantly preaching the values of peace, the pope in fact conducted a nonviolent religious war against tyrants.

• Lee Kwan Yu of Singapore took a country that was notorious for disease, poverty, and terrorism, and through single-minded rule and ruthless actions against his opponents transformed the tiny city-state into an island of creative energy and one of the most prosperous societies on earth.

• Lech Walesa of Poland used his own personal courage and the authority of the free trade union Solidarity to open a fatal fissure in the edifice of the Soviet Empire.

• Nelson Mandela of South Africa used his own personal courage and the authority of his rank as a tribal prince to break the will of the apartheid regime and, as Juan Carlos had done in Spain, led his nation peacefully to democracy.

• Margaret Thatcher of England broke the will of the English trade unions, revived the energies of her people, thrashed Argentina when the generals in Buenos Aires invaded British territory, and joined with two successive American presidents to defeat the enemies of the West, first the Soviet Empire and then Iraq in the Gulf War.

• Ronald Reagan of the United States, like Pope John Paul II, demonstrated personal courage in the face of an assassin, repeatedly defeated challenges to his authority at home, and led the successful campaign against the Soviet Empire. He defeated Soviet proxies on the battlefields of Afghanistan, Angola, and Grenada, cut off the Soviet Union from the crucial technologies of the West, and revived the flagging morale of the democracies to win the Cold War, the Third World War of the twentieth century.

These heroic figures, along with others like Vaclav Havel of Czechoslovakia, Mario Soares of Portugal, and Bettino Craxi of Italy, all understood that they had to assert their authority. Ronald Reagan's presidency was defined early on by a decisive exercise of power: the purge of the federal air controllers when they went on strike in 1981. From that moment on, both Reagan's domestic political opponents and the Soviets realized they were dealing with a tough guy. Margaret Thatcher dealt similarly with the British coal miners' union and earned her "Iron Lady" nickname. Mario Soares fought the Communists in the streets of Lisbon and Porto. John Paul II moved against early challenges from dissident priests, above all in the Jesuit order, to establish his authority within the Church. When a priest in Nicaragua joined the Communist government, the pope went to Managua, preached a sermon against godless tyranny, and ordered the priest to kneel and kiss the papal ring. Nelson Mandela drove would-be challengers— even his own wife—to the margins of power shortly after his release from captivity.

Many loved these leaders, but their authority was established in large part on fear, which grew as their enemies were decisively defeated or destroyed.

The next generation of leaders ignored their examples and sought public favor by catering to popular sentiment. From John Major to George Bush, from Jacques Chirac to Boutros Boutros-Ghali, the new leaders sought popularity and ignored the imperatives of rule. The Gulf War should have been the occasion to make Saddam Hussein an object lesson for any tyrant who contemplated attacking the West and its allies. Instead, Saddam was permitted to survive, and continued to plot revenge, convinced that he could do so without risking his rule. Subsequent events proved him right. The United States gave the United Nations authority to dismantle the Iraqi chemical, biological, and nuclear weapons programs, but the United Nations failed to do it, and by the beginning of 1998 most Western countries, having become convinced that the United States was not prepared to bring down Saddam's regime, were working toward normalizing relations with Iraq.

As shown earlier, this behavior is typical of what Machiavelli calls "effeminate states," nations that do not take seriously the requirements of international survival, led by men and women who have abandoned the ideals of virtue in favor of self-indulgence and a temporary popularity. Such leaders are often as impotent in their domestic conflicts as in the international arena. Take Newt Gingrich, who appeared for a moment to be a proper Machiavellian. In the 1994 elections, he organized the Republican party into a coherent fighting force and defined its mission, the "Contract with America," with near-military precision. He denounced the Democrats' corruption after more than forty years in control of the House of Representatives and attacked their liberal ideology as demeaning to enterprise, damaging to individual liberty, and ruinous for the nation's economic well-being. The Republican triumph was so great that many leading Democrats foresaw a generation of Republican rule. Yet in the next two years the Republicans were badly battered by Bill Clinton. He stole a march on Gingrich, adopting much of the Republicans' rhetoric, while attacking them as cruel and insensitive. Call it "Gingrichism with a human face." Gingrich steadily lost national prestige and the support of his own troops. Matters came to a head in July 1997, when a handful of Republican conspirators were caught plotting Gingrich's overthrow. Thus exposed, they were at Gingrich's mercy. Had he called for their removal from their positions of party power, he would certainly have prevailed. This in turn would have provided him the opportunity to reassert his leadership and revive Republican morale. Instead, he pretended that all was well, accepted the resignation of one conspirator, and left the remainder in place. It was the political equivalent of the Gulf

War. Like Bush, Gingrich failed to understand the importance of demonstrating the dire consequences of challenging his power, and risking public contempt. Similarly, John Major seemed utterly unable to make a basic decision on England's entry into the "new Europe," and became an object of ridicule. When Helmut Kohl of Germany dithered on reforming the welfare state, both supporters and opponents lost respect for him. All three were unceremoniously defeated, Gingrich by his own party, Major and Kohl by their national electorates. Machiavelli draws the general lesson:

> What makes [a leader] despised is being considered changeable, frivolous, effeminate, cowardly, irresolute; from these qualities a prince must guard himself as from a reef, and he must strive to make everyone recognize in his actions greatness, spirit, dignity, and strength.[15]

Machiavelli wants the kind of leader who follows the advice of Shaka, the late nineteenth century Zulu king who united his tribe and led them with great success against other regional forces, including the British Army. Shaka has passed into history as one of the greatest African monarchs and is much revered by his people, despite the great violence he used to unite the Zulus and defeat other tribes. He himself was in no doubt about the necessary basis for his rule. The Zulus, he said,

. . . are parts of two hundred and more unruly clans which I had to break up and reshape, and only the fear of death will hold them together. The time will come when they will be as one nation, and the clans will only be remembered as surnames. In the meantime my very name must inspire them with terror.[16]

Shaka fulfilled both his objectives and his prophecy. He would have no sympathy for contemporary leaders who find themselves abandoned by ungrateful supporters at a moment of weakness. His caustic remarks to a friend should be repeated to the current generation of leaders. "If I should put you in my place for the space of a moon, Zululand would fall to pieces; for with your stupid White man's reasoning you would first condone the little offenses."

Silvio Berlusconi of Italy paid scant attention to Machiavelli and foolishly followed "white man's reasoning," to his ruin. Having made his fortune in mass media and real estate, Berlusconi burst onto the political scene in 1994 with his newly minted movement, Forza Italia, and won the parliamentary election. His campaign contained themes strikingly similar to the Contract with America: lower taxes, smaller government, greater individual freedom. Berlusconi became prime minister at a potentially revolutionary moment, for the traditional parties had been gravely weakened by political and financial scandals that exposed a vast network of corruption involving politicians and businessmen. The Christian Democrats, the most powerful party in the country since the end of World War II, disappeared, as did the Socialists, who in the 1980s had been the primary coalition partners of the Christian Democrats. The opposition consisted of ex-Communists and a rump of Communist loyalists. Gravely weakened by their unexpected electoral defeat by Berlusconi, they purged their leaders and selected younger ones. Berlusconi seemed to be tailor-made for the situation, for he came from outside the discredited political class, and his political message, presented in carefully crafted sound bites designed by his media experts and broadcast over his television stations, resonated throughout the Italian body politic.

Berlusconi's greatest threat came from the judiciary, the instrument of the destruction of the old political parties and their corporate allies. Many judges made no secret of their political allegiance to the left and center-left parties and their consequent antipathy to Berlusconi and his movement. They were well versed in Machiavelli's methods. They ruthlessly used preventive detention as a means of extorting confessions from their targets. Innocent men were held for months on end without being charged and were informed that they would be released only if they gave the judges information that would permit action to be taken against more prominent politicians and businessmen.

It was obvious that if the judges were given the chance, the same methods would be used against Berlusconi and his allies. Accordingly, in 1995 the Berlusconi government introduced legislation to limit the use of preventive detention and bring the practice into line with the methods used elsewhere in Europe. Berlusconi's enemies, recognizing this to be a crucial test of will, filled the country's piazzas with hundreds of thousands of demonstrators, and a large segment of the media denounced the new laws and demanded they be withdrawn.

This battle determined Italy's domestic balance of power for a political generation. Under political siege, Berlusconi retreated. The proposed legislation was dropped. Shortly thereafter, on the occasion of an important international summit meeting in Italy, Berlusconi was publicly informed that he was under investigation for corruption. Over the succeeding months his prestige dropped steadily, and he was finally forced to step down. The triumphant judiciary relentlessly closed in on Berlusconi himself, his brother, and top officials of his business empire. The same methods were used to neutralize other potential opponents of the new center-left government, whose leaders were invariably spared any of the judicial ordeals that regularly afflicted the opposition.

Gingrich and Berlusconi failed in a way Machiavelli knows all too well; his own prince, Piero Soderini, did the same thing. Soderini was elected lifetime leader of the Florentine republic in 1502, after a bitter struggle between those who wanted an aristocracy and the supporters of a more popular form of government. Soderini was the candidate of the populists, and the aristocrats fought him from the beginning of his tenure. In September 1512, following a military defeat, Soderini's government was overthrown by his enemies, who called for the return of the Medici. Machiavelli's description of Soderini's downfall fits both our contemporary examples:

> [Soderini] believed that, with the passage of time, with goodness and with his own good luck and the occasional gift, he would be able to overcome the jealousy of [his enemies]. . . . However, he was quite young . . . and although his natural sagacity recognized the necessity of destroying them, and although the quality and ambition of his adversaries afforded him the opportunity, yet he had not the courage to do it. . . . He was the dupe of his opinions, not knowing that malignity is neither effaced by time, nor placated by gifts. Thus . . . he lost at the same time his country, his state, and his reputation.[17]

Neither Gingrich nor Berlusconi has vanished from politics, but they cannot hope to recover the grandeur of their days of triumph. Their enemies will not fear them, and the people will remain contemptuous, although probably not as intensely as

Machiavelli was of his former leader. When Soderini died, Machiavelli penned a terrible epigram:

> The night Soderini died
> his spirit descended to the mouth of hell;
> Pluto shouted: "But what hell? Foolish spirit
> Get yourself to limbo with the other children."[18]

By contrast, Bill Clinton (who, to put it mildly, greatly prefers being loved to being feared), gives no quarter to his domestic political opponents. Notoriously attentive to the details of the political struggle, Clinton used every available method to damage the opposition. By mid-1997, the Internal Revenue Service had opened audits on at least twenty non-profit organizations that were hostile to Clinton, while none friendly to the administration was known to be under investigation. In one case, apparently an innovation, the IRS began its investigation even before an audit had begun (the group, Fortress America, were so new it hadn't had time to file an income tax return). A lawyer for one of the groups accurately observed, "[Clinton] cares about power and he's using the most feared enforcement tool in the government to attack people who are opposing him politically. He's using government to achieve personal political goals."[19]

Indecisive in international affairs, Clinton nonetheless understands the domestic uses of power and exercises it with manifest skill and satisfaction. No president in recent memory has fought so tenaciously and effectively against his political opponents. His tactical strokes against his various accusers and investigators in Congress and the judiciary were masterful for several years; unlike Nixon and Reagan before him, he long managed to block the release of potentially damaging information, and he maintained effective control over his own people. But mastery of technique would not have been sufficient to endear him to Machiavelli, for whom the most important thing is virtuous behavior in behalf of the common good. To use Machiavelli's methods to simply maintain personal power without fighting for the basic principles on which any successful enterprise is built is a dangerous perversion of Machiavelli's requirements for good leadership. It is, as an Italian editorialist recently commented "Machiavellism without Machiavelli," and observed:

> The great political essayists did indeed speak of the advantages of dissimulation, but only if it was "honest," only if it incorporated some realistic high-mindedness. Machiavellism without Machiavelli is an inedible theoretical and practical stew. Without the saucy pulp of a political goal, embraced and loved with passion, almost like an act of faith, tricks are just tricks, often painful expedients of the sort best carried out by the amoral frauds that abound in the alleys of the city.[20]

A good state can be effectively led only by a virtuous leader who effectively uses his power for advancing the goals of the nation rather than for his own personal aggrandizement. When leaders become corrupt, when they become notoriously lascivious and indolent, shrink from international conflict, and subvert the political process for their own advancement, they threaten the entire enterprise with corruption.

The corruption of a virtuous state is not unusual (indeed, it's the rule), and it typically occurs at moments of great success, just when the nation feels itself strong and secure. Machiavelli writes of such a moment in ancient Rome.

[The Romans] were secure of their liberty, and did not see any enemies who could frighten them. This security and the weakness of their enemies induced the Romans to name Consuls not on the basis of virtue, but of popularity, elevating to those high offices men who knew how to charm the people, not those who knew how to defeat their enemies; then, later, from those most charming they descended to those most powerful, so that the good men . . . were completely excluded.[21]

This corruption undermined the republican institutions that had produced the grandeur of Rome, and weakened the nation to the point that her enemies could threaten her very existence. Our danger today is the same. Lulled into security by the weakness of our enemies, comforted by the wealth created by our industry, our leaders are sliding into the mire Machiavelli knows so well and detests so intensely. He believes he knows how to deal with it.

Do we?

CHAPTER  SIX

FREEDOM

For it is as difficult to make a people free that is resolved
to live in servitude, as it is to subject a people to servitude that is determined to be free.

Moses led the Israelites out of Egypt, through the Red Sea,
and across the Sinai Peninsula. After receiving the Ten Commandments and crushing the heretics worshiping the golden
calf, he continued on to the borders of the Promised Land.
There, at God's instructions, Moses organized a reconnais-
sance mission headed by Joshua and Caleb, in preparation for
the invasion and occupation of the country. After forty days
the spies returned. The good news was that the land was beautiful and bountiful; the bad news was that the inhabitants were
big and strong, impressively armed, and well fortified. All the
spies save Joshua and Caleb argued that it was suicidal to attack, and the vast majority of the people agreed. Fearing they

were about to be destroyed in battle, they turned against Moses. "And they said one to another: 'Let us appoint a captain, and let us return into Egypt.'" Recently freed from Egyptian slavery, the Israelites nonetheless demanded a return to bondage rather than fight for freedom.

This was the beginning of a vast revolt against Moses, a revolt that spread to every tribe and involved the most powerful and distinguished leaders as well as members of the priestly hierarchy, and even Aaron himself. Some accused Moses of abuse of power, while others denounced him for incompetence. As at Mount Sinai, the participants were ruthlessly punished. The ringleaders were killed, and God sentenced the remainder of the adults to die wandering in the wilderness for forty years, a year for each of the days of the espionage mission. Of the adults, only Joshua and Caleb were permitted to enter the Promised Land and live there in freedom.

The revolt against Moses in the name of slavery is one of the most powerful of the "infinite examples" to which Machiavelli refers in order to show the difficulties in leading a people to freedom that has become accustomed to living under dictatorship. Such people, he tells us, are no different from a wild animal raised in captivity. Knowing neither how to feed itself nor find sanctuary, in the wild the tamed beast falls easy prey to its enemies. In like manner, people entering democracy after being raised under dictatorship, "not knowing how to reason about defense or public offenses . . . quickly returns under the yoke, most often worse than the one they had recently lifted from their necks."[1] The metaphor has had a long life, as readers of the *Washington Post* discovered not so long ago.

> "Some people find it hard to bear the responsibility of freedom," said Jaroslava Moserova, vice president of the Czech Senate. "I call it the zoo concept. When the doors to the zoo are opened and the animals set free, it is the predators who make the best use of their newfound liberty. The timid ones . . . find it safer to go back behind bars."[2]

Moreover, Machiavelli notes, a leader of a new democracy has to contend with the enmity of all those who profited from the dictatorship. They resent a free society in which "honors and rewards [are given] according to honest and specific reasons, and otherwise no one is rewarded or honored."

So it was with the Israelites. Not Moses, not even God himself, could overcome the slave mentality of the Jews who grew up under Egyptian tyranny. To create a free nation, that entire generation had to be obliterated in the wilderness. A new generation, raised in freedom, fulfilled the mission.

If the Israelites, blessed with superb (indeed, divine) leadership, needed two generations to accomplish the transition to freedom, why should we be surprised to see the former slave states of the Soviet Empire, with their mediocre and timorous leaders, struggling to establish the rule of law and the habits and responsibilities of freedom? The return to power of the former Communist elites is the contemporary version of the demand of the Israelites to be taken back to Egypt. Machiavelli would have predicted that the most successful contemporary transitions from democracy to dictatorship would occur in countries like Spain and Portugal, where the dictatorships were relatively mild, or the tyranny was of short duration, as in the Baltic and Central European satellites, which fell under the Soviet yoke only after the Second World War. The Baltic and Central European satellites have done better than Russia, Georgia, Belarus, and the Ukraine, which were subjected to the Bolshevik tyranny early in the century.

Machiavelli reminds us that people's capacity for freedom is intimately linked to their history. Unfortunately, our children no longer hear this in their schools—the requirement that no one's history be criticized having recently taken precedence over the quaint notion of simply telling the story. Our current desire to believe that all peoples are fundamentally the same blinds us to this reality. It also makes good leadership more difficult. If the leaders of the West had appreciated the damage done to the human spirit by nearly a century of totalitarian rule, they would have better understood the enormous difficulties facing the nations of the old Soviet Union. They should have imposed more draconian requirements—including the purge of the old elites, the establishment of the rule of law establishing sanctity of private property and contracts, for example—in exchange for material assistance, just as we did with the vanquished fascist nations after the Second World War. Good laws and good institutions are two of the three legs of the good state.

The most successful new democracies after both World War II and the Cold War had a tradition of freedom, a pool of virtue to draw upon after the defeat of the tyrants. As Machiavelli explains: "In republics there is greater vitality, greater hatred, greater desire for revenge; the memory of ancient liberty never leaves."[3] So great is the power of free traditions that Machiavelli advises would-be conquerors of free states to destroy or scatter the inhabitants, because otherwise they will never forget "the spirit of liberty and [their] ancient institutions." Stalin tried precisely that, murdering and relocating tens of millions of people in a desperate attempt to eradicate their historical memories, but even he was unable to fully overcome the spirit of liberty among peoples like the Chechens.

But no matter how strong the old traditions of liberty, it is hard for people to learn to make their own decisions after they have become accustomed to act only when directed to do so. This is as true in business as in politics, as was discovered by the ambitious and idealistic leaders who transformed United Airlines from dictatorship to democracy. United had followed the usual "top-down" corporate model, and, like the rest of the airlines, ran into hard times in the early 1990s. Conflict between management and the various unions was so intense that they were unable to agree on a restructuring plan. The impasse was resolved by a cultural revolution within United. In the summer of 1994, the company's new CEO, Gerald Greenwald, negotiated the business equivalent of a transition from dictatorship to democracy. In exchange for nearly $5 billion in wage concessions over the next five and a half years, United gave 55 percent of its shares to participating employees. The hope was that the workers would be better motivated if their income increased along with corporate profits.

Greenwald was well suited to this challenge, having played a lead role in turning around Chrysler in the late 1970s, thereby gaining a reputation as a "workers' champion." But Greenwald knew that a change in ownership, even if it produced a profound improvement in staff morale, would not be enough. United's methods seemed almost designed to frustrate initiative. The new president, John Edwardson, found that he had to approve purchase requests from a vice president for anything in excess of $4,999. "Is this a joke?" he asked, "or are you testing me?" It was neither, simply business as usual in a $12 billion company struggling to keep its head above water. Predictably, the company had not had four consecutive profitable quarters since 1989.

United needed a fundamental transformation of the way it did business, at every level. The new leaders' first requirement was to make it possible for people with hands-on knowledge of the problems to tackle them directly, without having to clear their actions through layers of bureaucracy.

Greenwald accordingly moved quickly to give greater authority all the way down the line: the old limit of $500,000 for construction contracts was raised tenfold to $5 million. The old ceiling on the discretionary authority of the vice president for purchasing went from $750,000 to $5 million. In the past, the vice president for cargo could sign contracts up to a million dollars, and only for a year at a time. The ceiling went up to $10 million and five years. The CFO had been limited to $25 million; all limits were removed. At the same time, entire layers of supervisory bureaucracy were removed. More than one hundred supervisors were offered other positions (with no drop in salary), and employees at all levels were told, "If you have a problem and know how to solve it, just do it."

It was easier said than done, because employees were not accustomed to making decisions on their own. They had been paid to follow instructions, and if things worked out badly, they were not held accountable. Now they had been given greater freedom, but freedom carries obligations. They would be judged and rewarded by their results: praises, raises, and promotions if they succeeded, but criticism and reduced authority if they made things worse. Greenwald, Edwardson, and other top officers spent half their time trying to inculcate the new culture directly to their employees on the runways and in the kitchens, ticket offices, and maintenance hangars.

Greenwald well understood Machiavelli's emphasis on the importance of dramatically staged events in instilling virtue in the people, and three early events helped inspire the employees. First was the launch of a new shuttle on the West Coast between Los Angeles and San Francisco, planned and implemented by over a hundred United employees. A steering committee was originally formed by top management to develop a time frame for their project, but it quickly stepped aside to let the people on the ground make the operational decisions. These were taken largely by shuttle teams in each airport, which hammered out policies in twice-a-day meetings.

The second dramatic action was the decentralization of key decision making from corporate headquarters to major cities. Previously, as James Goodwin, the senior vice president for North America, put it:

We never, ever shared with our people at a given location the profitability of their business entity. Consequently, people . . . have a cost target and they make it . . . and we reward them. . . . And the sales organization is making sales quotas and we're patting them on the back.

But we're losing our shirt. So we come along one day and line the employees up against a wall and say: "You all have done a fine job. We just can't make any money here and we're going to close. . . ." And you've got 30 stunned people.[4]

Under the new culture, major cities were given responsibility for their entire program, so that everyone involved understood all the ingredients that went into United's business. Within seven months, the first test program was in the black.

The third dramatic change at United was a CEO with virtue. Instead of pretending that everything was going well, he announced early on that the airline industry, including United, had been "full of smoke and clouds and nobody believes us anymore." He readily admitted that flying was not a glamorous experience; seats were too small, lines at check-in and ticket counters were too long, and the food was dreadful. He promised United would make things better. New planes would be more comfortable, new electronic ticketing would soon be online, food quality would improve. And it happened.

The results of Gerald Greenwald's cultural revolution at United were spectacular. Employee morale soared, as is demonstrated by a steady fall in lost time from injuries and sick leave. Sick leave in 1995 may well stand as a barometer of United's turnaround: down 7.4 percent in March, down 10 percent in April, down 18.8 percent in May from the previous year. Employee complaints were down more than 80 percent in the same period, at the same time that United achieved the lowest unit cost of the three major carriers in the country. Given greater freedom, United's employees had worked harder and had advanced the common good.

The bottom line showed the same progress. The company was profitable less than a year after the employee takeover, and by the first anniversary Greenwald was able to announce a 67 percent gain in the value of United common stock, amounting to an increase of $1.9 billion in the value of the company. In the spring of 1996, United announced a four-for-one stock split. By late 1997, United shares had gone up a dazzling 260 percent.

In one of those many paradoxes Machiavelli understands so well, Greenwald found that the empowerment of United's employees and the decentralization of a great deal of corporate decision making had not weakened his authority, but actually increased it. No head of government is as powerful as the leader of a free people, provided that he proves his commitment to the common good. The same applies to business.

Machiavelli would insist on drawing a further lesson from the success at United. Greenwald had proved to be an exceptional leader, but he was able to unleash the creative initiative of his employees in such a short time because they came from a free society. Their initiative had been stifled by the authoritarian methods of previous corporate leaders, but once they saw that they were not being tricked, but truly were being offered greater freedom, they knew how to accept it. Such a rapid change is not possible within businesses in societies that have long been unfree, as Greenwald himself discovered in a stint as CEO at Tatra, the Czech vehicle manufacturer, just before becoming CEO of United. In such countries the transition to freedom, even within the freest corporate atmosphere, may take a generation or more.

There is thus one final paradox: the notion of workers' ownership of the means of production was a staple of socialist ideology, but it failed in the Soviet Bloc because of the lack of freedom in both the marketplace and civil society. Instead, it has succeeded in the heart of democratic capitalism, which offers the greatest freedom.

CORRUPTION

If the spirit of liberty is so strong, why do free nations and enterprises fall, and dictators arise from their ruin? Machiavelli lays the blame on corrupt leaders, and then the corruption of the people themselves. "To usurp supreme and absolute authority . . . in a free state, and subject it to tyranny, the people must have already become corrupt by gradual steps from generation to generation."[5] Once that has happened, the enterprise is probably doomed. Free societies depend upon the virtue of the people; there is a symbiotic relationship between the good laws and institutions upon which the enterprise rests, and the virtuous behavior of the citizens. Just as "good laws are necessary to maintain good customs, so good customs are necessary for good laws to be observed."[6] Weaken the one, and the other slides down into corruption, with terrible consequences: the indolence and selfishness that destroys even the greatest human achievements. Once the rot sets in, even the finest institutions are useless. "Neither laws nor constitutional systems are sufficient to rein in a general corruption."

Machiavelli uses two of our most cherished rights—freedom of expression and freedom of assembly—to demonstrate the intimate connection between a virtuous citizenry and the proper functioning of a free state. If the people are devoted to the common good and committed to the rule of law, then even the most tumultuous protest is a positive action, for it reflects concern that the leaders have deviated from just principles. But if the people have been corrupted, if the bulk of the citizens are more interested in personal gain than in the general welfare, then riots and other disturbances are threatening to the state. Free and open debate is invaluable when men are virtuous, but dangerous when they are corrupt, because great orators, advocating measures that advance only their own gain, often carry the day. Further: So long as the state is sound, citizens will freely express their opinions, to the benefit of all. But once the rot has set in, honest men and women will be afraid to speak openly, knowing that they are likely to be the targets of those whom they criticize.

Free enterprises, whether businesses or teams, families or nations, must relentlessly fight corruption. On Wall Street, where incredible sums of money are handled every working day, the best firms go to extraordinary lengths to catch employees playing fast and loose with the rules. At Bear Stearns, for example, the trading floor is populated not only with genuine traders and their assistants but also "moles"—watchers paid by the firm to spy on the traders and to report any hint of financial irregularities, drug or alcohol use, or other unacceptable behavior. The moles act just like the traders, so that they are indistinguishable from their colleagues, but their existence is well known, thereby enhancing the effect. And when improper actions are found, the malefactors are quickly demoted or dismissed, no matter how great their past contributions to the firm. As Machiavelli insists,

No well-ordered republic ever canceled its citizens' demerits with their merits. . . . Having rewarded a citizen for performing well, if the selfsame man does evil he must be punished without any regard for his good works. And when these fundamental principles are well enforced, a [nation] lives free for a long time: otherwise it is quickly ruined.[7]

Both virtue and corruption flow from the top down (leaders are *not* corrupted by the people, although they often blame their own failure on their followers). The Ecuadorian political leader Alberto Dahik has remarked, brutally, "When the perception is that corruption begins at the top, everything falls into decay. If the minister himself steals, the undersecretaries will commit assaults and the departmental directors will engage in theft, extortion, robbery, and murder."[8]

Leaders must therefore personify the virtues expected of the others (or at least must be perceived to be virtuous). One of the stories that best defines the virtuous culture of Bear Stearns is about the former CEO and current chairman, Allen "Ace" Greenberg. Coming into La Guardia Airport after an exhausting business trip, a junior executive accompanying Greenberg happily informed him that there was a limousine waiting at the exit. "What's wrong?" Greenberg asked, "are the Yellow Cabs on strike?"

To ward off corruption, the enterprise must be constantly renewed and reinvigorated, ideally by a dramatic application of good laws and the behavior of good leaders, thereby re-asserting its basic virtues. Machiavelli believes this should be done at least every ten years, because a decade suffices for leaders and populace to stray from the principles that made the enterprise successful in the first place. To wait longer invites grave degeneration; "Men begin to change their habits and to transgress the laws, and if their memory of punishment is not refreshed, and fear is not renewed in their spirit, soon so many delinquents will be found that they cannot be punished without danger."[9]

The nature of the remedy will vary according to the virulence of the disease in the body politic. Generally, a dramatic action will be needed to reassert the good state's first principles, for example taking a powerful figure and subjecting him to merciless punishment or destruction; or passing a new law that cracks down on those who violate or undermine the state's basic norms and principles; or elevating to a position of great power one who has shown exemplary devotion to the founding principles of the enterprise. A good constitution, updated with good laws that "oblige the citizens often to render an account of their conduct," provides a sound foundation for renewal, but here, as always, good leadership is indispensable. "To give life and vigor to those laws requires a virtuous citizen, who will courageously aid in their execution against the power of those who transgress them."[10]

Machiavelli writes enthusiastically about the punishment or execution of corrupt persons, best of all if they are carried out in a spectacular manner so as to drive home the message to the people. He knew at first hand of a particularly dramatic execution, carried out by Cesare Borgia in 1502. Borgia had just conquered the province of Romagna and found it wildly out of control. Brigands commanded the roads, thieves and murderers operated freely in the cities, and civil authority had disintegrated. To restore order, Borgia dispatched his trusted aide, Ramiro de Lorqua, and made him president of the region. De Lorqua brutally established control. He rounded up dozens of criminals and had them executed, and the slightest infraction of the laws was quickly punished. This was rule by fear, with a vengeance. Then, without any hint to prepare them, the citizens of Cesena found a shocking spectacle in the central piazza of the capital. The body of de Lorqua, split in two, lay on display, next to a bloody knife. "The ferocity of such a spectacle," Machiavelli remarks, "left those people simultaneously satisfied and stupefied."

Contemporary leaders, with their tendency to forgive everyone for everything, would do well to ponder the wisdom of Machiavelli's lesson on the importance of punishment of major malefactors, especially when it is dramatically inflicted. He well understands the doubly valuable psychological effect on the people. First of all, they are awed by the violence of the act, which brings low a mighty figure. This shows them that even the most powerful are subject to justice under the law, and it reminds them of the power—Borgia's, in Machiavelli's spectacular example—to punish anyone who performs a criminal act. The second psychological element is "satisfaction," the kind of catharsis the audience undergoes while watching a classic tragedy. The Medicis acted in this way when the Pazzi tried to destroy them, and their memorable acts of vengeance provided all Florentines with a most satisfying spectacle.

Our periodic purges of corrupt politicians are just the sort of thing he has in mind, whether Watergate or Whitewater in America, the destruction of the old political class in Italy, or the humiliation of politicians and managers in Japan. Nowadays we generally destroy men's reputations and careers rather than taking their lives (outside Asia there are very few suicides of public figures although there were a few in Italy), but the effect on the public is the same, especially as many of our most deadly modern executioners are journalists and broadcasters who provide the necessary stage and bring the drama to a large audience. Nothing so effectively reminds the people that their leaders must act within legal limits as incarcerating some powerful men who believed they were above the law, or destroying them by scandal.

The Contract with America, leading to the savage electoral

punishment of the Democratic party, meets Machiavelli's standards, as do the periodic "great awakenings" that unleash waves of religious fervor and then creative political vigor. American evangelical Christianity is the sort of "good religion" Machiavelli calls for. The evangelicals do not quietly accept their destiny, believing instead they are called upon to fight corruption and reestablish virtue. American political institutions, and the cyclical religious revivals that seem part of our national DNA, help explain the durability of the republic.

> Those are the best constituted bodies, and have the longest existence, which possess the intrinsic means of frequently renewing themselves. . . . For, as all . . . must have within themselves some goodness, by means of which they obtain their first expansion and reputation, and as in the process of time this goodness because corrupted, it will of necessity destroy the body unless something intervenes to bring it back to its normal condition.[11]

Of course, we can always get lucky. Stunning events from outside can providentially awaken the enterprise from its growing torpor, and demonstrate the need for renewal, as the devastating Japanese attack on Pearl Harbor in 1941 so effectively aroused the United States from its soothing dreams of permanent neutrality, and as the revelations of Alexandr Solzhenitsyn, Vladimir Bukovsky, and the other eloquent Soviet dissidents aroused the West in the last phase of the Cold War. American business was similarly shocked out of its lethargy in the early eighties by the competitive attacks of Japanese products, from automobiles to electronics. Thanks to those devastating assaults, American corporations were forced to renew themselves, redesign their products, increase their productivity, and restructure their organizations. Without the foreign challenge, the great American economic accomplishments of the past fifteen years would not have taken place.

But we cannot count on competitors and enemies to save us; it is only a matter of time before we face a serious crisis. Corruption *does* come in; it is already there, in our nature, awaiting its opportunity. And the opportunity will always arise, typically just when things look best. Basking in false security, we drop our guard. If the enterprise is not renewed in time, the rot spreads, corrupting the entire society.

Of the countless examples of great empires that sealed their doom by abandoning virtue just when things seemed most glorious, the decline of the Ottoman Empire was perhaps best understood at the time it actually happened. The Ottoman Turks reached their zenith in the middle of the sixteenth century under the leadership of one of history's greatest rulers,

Suleyman the Magnificent. Precisely at that moment, Lutfi Pasha, Suleyman's retired grand vizier, saw the first terrible steps that led down the road to corruption. He saw the usual fatal mistakes: "venality and incompetence; the multiplication of a useless and wasteful army and bureaucracy; the vicious circle of financial stringency, fiscal rapacity, and economic strangulation; the decay of integrity and loyalty; and beyond them all, the growing, menacing shadow of the maritime states of the West."[12]

Lutfi Pasha called upon Suleyman to return to the principles that had made the empire great, appealing to him above all to exercise his personal power and prestige against the growing spread of favoritism in important appointments. It was not to be. By the middle of the next century, Sultan Murad IV's chief adviser, Kochu Bey—often called the Turkish Montesquieu, for the elegance and subtlety of his thought—wrote a devastating memorandum on the state of the empire. The main points of his critique could form the basis for a manual of Machiavelli's "thou-shalt-nots" for leaders:

- The sultans had withdrawn from direct supervision of the state.

- The office of grand vizier, the number two position, had been debased by making it a political appointment, and therefore "subjected to all kinds of interference by palace favorites and liable at any moment to summary dismissal, confiscation, and even execution."

• Other key positions, including membership in the elite corps of the armed forces, had become available to anyone willing to pay a suitable bribe, and "appointment to office by purchase or favor had become general—even in religious offices such as judgeships."

If corruption brought down the Ottoman Empire, it can easily destroy less glorious enterprises. The wisdom of Machiavelli's profound concern about corruption has recently been rediscovered by the world's leading financial institutions.

The International Monetary Fund and the World Bank are bluntly telling developing countries with bad governments to stamp out graft or lose the money. For the first time, bankers are openly challenging politicians. . . .

In the 50 countries he has visited, [World Bank President James] Wolfensohn said, "Corruption is the biggest issue on the minds of voters and the single largest inhibiting factor" for private investment.[13]

Notably, Wolfensohn's remarks were made before the onset of the Asian financial crisis, which revealed far greater corruption than anyone had guessed. The model for the crisis was Japan, which by the mid-1990s had fallen prey to the sort of moral and intellectual rot that Machiavelli warns about. Instead of giving increased opportunity to their people, who are widely admired as being the best-educated in the world, the Japanese elite insisted upon a high degree of central planning. Major corporate decisions were rarely taken freely by company officials, but were more often negotiated with government planners, other captains of industry, a plethora of in-house bankers and trade union leaders, and the ubiquitous national mafia. Competition was moderated and in some cases eliminated in favor of a negotiated consensus within the industrial/financial community or of outright instructions from the planners. Workers were rewarded for their cooperation with virtually guaranteed lifetime contracts. The impressive growth of Japanese industry, particularly from the mid-seventies on, convinced many in Asia and the West that the American model had been overtaken by "Asian capitalism" and that any country that did not adopt Japanese methods was doomed to failure. They had not only forgotten Machiavelli's warning that things are constantly changing, but they had ignored his commentary that great enterprises are created by the few, but best maintained by the many.

Many Japanese embraced the same illusion. Japanese bankers, egged on by the central planners, made substantial loans to enterprises that weren't worth the risk. As always, an intimate relationship between government and business produces the corruption of both: Government officials failed to insist on proper standards, in part because they received substantial kickbacks from bankers, industrialists, and mafiosi. Like the highly leveraged "pyramids" of the United States stock market in the twenties, much of the Japanese boom in the eighties and early nineties was the result of creative accounting practices and connivance, not an increase in real value. Foreign investors followed suit, and by the early 1990s, the market value of real estate in downtown Tokyo was higher than that of all the real estate in the United States. This was the so-called "bubble economy." Like the American stock market on the eve of the great crash of 1929, the system worked well as long as new money continued to pour in, but the entire structure collapsed once investors decided to cash out. When the bubble burst in the mid- and late nineties, real estate values dropped by over 60 percent, and the yen lost 40 percent of its value. As lenders scrambled to protect their assets, it was discovered that many American and European banks had made substantial loans without even examining the balance sheets of their creditors. The pattern was repeated in other Asian countries, from Thailand and Indonesia to Korea.

The Asian lending frenzy was every bit as irrational, and every bit as corrupt, as any of the famous speculative booms in history, like the Dutch tulip frenzy of the seventeenth century. The lust for rare specimens of these flowers drove prices for tulip bulbs to the skies, and created in microcosm a complete market system, from "puts" and "calls" to governmental regulatory agencies. Toward the end of the boom, strong-arm tactics were regularly employed by ambitious men attempting to corner the market on rare bulbs and flowers.

A shoemaker of the Hague . . . finally managed to grow a black [tulip]. He was visited by some growers from Haarlem, to whom he sold his treasure for 1,500 florins. Immediately one of them dropped it to the floor and stamped on it until it was ground to pulp. The cobbler was aghast. The buyers explained that they, too, possessed a black tulip, and had destroyed his to protect the uniqueness of their own. They would have paid anything: 10,000 florins, if necessary. The heartbroken cobbler is said to have died of chagrin.[14]

The archetypal fraudulent boom was the so-called "Ponzi scheme," named after the Italian immigrant who in the nineteen twenties offered constantly rising interest rates to investors, thereby kicking off a torrent of investment that enabled him to pay off the original lenders with recently arrived money. Japanese real estate and financial markets were a modern-day version of Ponzi's operation. The whole operation was greased by payoffs to key decision makers in both business and government.

The frenzy was also encouraged by a more subtle form of corruption at a higher level. International financial institutions like the World Bank and International Monetary Fund repeatedly covered the losses of private banks in distressed countries, most recently in Mexico in 1995. Instead of insisting that governments, banks, and corporations be held accountable for their reckless actions, the World Bank and the IMF made low-interest loans to the threatened countries so that all debts to lenders could be paid. Lenders were thereby corrupted by what the economists elegantly call "moral hazard":

> When [there are] guarantees that some or all of an institution's losses will be shifted to taxpayers (through underpriced insurance, IMF bailout, or other safety-net guarantees), while gains will be kept by the institution's owners, the institution will be led to take excessive risks.[15]

Indeed, questions of risk were often totally ignored by the banks. And why not? If your losses are going to be covered, either by local governments or by the giant international institutions, there is no reason for prudence. In such a system, where you can gain or break even, but never lose, corruption is inevitable. Instead of looking for the best risk or the most promising investment, those with money will look for the highest bidder.

Machiavelli would condemn the Asian bailout (hastily organized by the IMF and its major contributors) because the corrupt people who produced the disaster were not punished, but were left in place. Unlike a bankruptcy sale, which would have removed many of the failed lenders and managers, the IMF bailout took money from the taxpayers of the successful countries and redistributed it to the corrupt enterprises and their creditors. One does not encourage virtue by taxing the virtuous to pay the costs of the sinful. One does it by punishing the sinful.

Investors, like voters, will always make mistakes, and markets are as vulnerable as electorates to excesses of enthusiasm. But in economics as in politics, the best hope for rational behavior is accountability to a large number of people. Elites, as Machiavelli observes, too often substitute their personal interests for the common good, which is why he prefers republics to monarchies and why market economies—the economic equivalent of political democracy—are superior to central planning. In the Asian affair, in 1997 the United States government blocked a Japanese plan to have the nations of the region deal with the crisis themselves—a plan that would have saved American taxpayers tens of billions of dollars. A year later the Americans called for the massive IMF bailout. The former Federal Reserve governor Lawrence Lindsey reported being told by a senior European central banker that "the only reason [the banker] could find for the U.S. refusal to cooperate was that [American] Treasury officials wanted to be seen playing a role." Lindsey acidly remarked, "U.S. contributions to a bailout may have as much to do with bureaucratic empire-building as with solving an economic crisis."[16] Machiavelli puts it in its starkest form: "The excesses of the people are directed against those whom they suspect of interfering with the public good; whilst those of princes are against those feared of interfering with their individual interests."[17]

Machiavelli was thus quite right to contend that the people are better suited to maintaining a good state than is a single ruler. The public is usually less corrupt than the leaders, and is far more concerned about corruption than the elites are. People can be deceived by clever charlatans, but Machiavelli thinks that, for the most part, the people are far more likely to choose virtuous leaders. Nonetheless, given the rottenness of human nature, the popular choice of corrupt leaders is a constant threat, even to virtuous democracies. Alexis de Tocqueville knew that

> . . . what is to be feared is not so much the immorality of the great as the fact that immorality may lead to greatness. . . . [The people] are . . . led, and often rightly, to

impute [a leader's] success mainly to some of his vices; and an odious connection is thus formed between the ideas of turpitude and power, unworthiness and success, utility and dishonor.

If the people believe their leaders achieve power *because* they are corrupt, it means that the entire enterprise has been discredited. Once the "odious connection between the ideas of turpitude and power" is established in the public mind, corruption will spread like wildfire. All those powerful passions Machiavelli understands so well overwhelm the virtuous laws and institutions, and the common good is smothered in the quest for more. And, as Tocqueville continues, while such dirty secrets can often be concealed in a dictatorship, they quickly emerge in free societies:

> The people can never penetrate into the dark labyrinth of court intrigue, and will always have difficulty in detecting the turpitude that lurks under elegant manners, refined tastes, and graceful language. But to pillage the public purse and to sell the favors of the state are arts that the meanest villain can understand and hope to practice in his turn.[18]

We recognize this language; it is our daily bread. The deadly connection between power and turpitude is now deeply ingrained in the minds of citizens throughout the free nations of the world. In America, hardly a week goes by without new examples of the systematic corruption of the political class, beginning with President Clinton and his closest associates. In India, so many politicians are being dragged to trial that there is now a "party of the guilty." Mexico spawns one corrupt administration after another. The former Italian prime minister Silvio Berlusconi is facing trial in Milan, and former prime minister Giulio Andreotti is on trial in Palermo. The Spanish prime minister, Felipe Gonzales, was compelled to schedule the early elections that ended his long tenure because of allegations of financial and antiterrorist wrongdoing. French politicians and businessmen across the political spectrum have been destroyed by judges, and in Belgium two former foreign ministers fell to investigations into political payoffs from military contracts (one, Willy Claes, lost the post of NATO secretary general). The government of Prime Minister John Major of Britain became a virtual laughingstock after many of its leading lights were forced to resign because of financial and sexual transgressions. Prime Minister Oleksy of Poland was forced to resign during investigations into his previous KGB connections, and President Santer of Colombia called for an investigation into his own campaign's financing. Former officials of South Africa's military intelligence service have been brought to trial, along with the ex-president, P. W. Botha, and there are mounting calls for investigations of Nelson Mandela's African National Congress. The world's most scandal-ridden country, Japan, lurches from one grotesque revelation to the next as once-untouchable politicians and business leaders come and go with startling frequency, sometimes taking their own lives because of the shame of it all. Former and current top officials and business leaders are standing trial in South Korea, and a wave of suicides accompanied parliamentary investigations into corruption in Taiwan. Russia may be the first major country to fall completely under the control of organized crime, and even in China, with the instruments of repression still largely intact, accusations of corruption in high places are becoming more frequent. The former presidents of Peru and Venezuela are facing trial, and the authority of President Fujimori of Peru has been undermined by scandal. Scandinavian political leaders' half-life diminishes by the month. In America, two Democratic and one Republican Speakers of the House of Representatives have fallen from power as a result of scandal, and former Speaker Gingrich paid a large sum in a negotiated settlement based on Ethics Committee findings of wrongdoing.

As corruption or charges of corruption mount, the people clamor for retribution, hoping the rot can be swept away. Leaders are implored to weed out corruption and restore the nation to virtue. Kochu Bey called upon the sultan to reassert his authority, purge the evildoers, and restore virtue. "On the Day of Judgment," he implored, "not ministers, but kings will be asked for a reckoning, and it will be no answer for them to say to the Lord of the Worlds, 'I delegated this duty.'" But pleading for reform to the leader of a corrupt enterprise is like asking the madam to institute chastity in her bordello. The rot starts at the top and cannot be cured by the corrupt leaders themselves. New leaders with an iron will are required to root out the corruption and either reestablish a virtuous state, or institute a new one.

For all his admiration of the wisdom of the people, Machiavelli fears that democracy will have to be sacrificed if freedom is to be rescued.

THE NEW PRINCE

Once corruption has taken hold of a free nation, it is headed toward tyranny. The delicate and vital relationship between good traditions and good laws is broken, and leaders seeking their own personal aggrandizement take over. The very issue of virtue is driven from public discourse. Those who doubt the accuracy of Machiavelli's analysis should consider the American presidential elections of 1996, in which the Republican candidates, Bob Dole and Jack Kemp, announced with apparent satisfaction that they would not make the "character" of

Bill Clinton an issue in the campaign. Refusing to hold public officials accountable for their corrupt practices reinforces the people's perception that turpitude and power are inextricably linked, and undermines even the best laws and institutions. Inevitably, with the passage of time, liberty itself is crushed.

In a corrupt state, Machiavelli grimly observes, even "the best laws are of no avail, unless they are administered by a man of such supreme power that he may cause the laws to be observed until the mass has been restored to a healthy condition."[19] Only a strong, resolute, and virtuous leader can save the enterprise from ruin. Paradoxically, preserving liberty may require the rule of a single leader—a dictator—willing to use those dreaded "extraordinary measures, which few know how, or are willing, to employ." We hardly need to be reminded of the infamous list of extraordinary measures: a leader in such drastic circumstances "will often be compelled in order to preserve the state to work against good faith, against charity, against humaneness, against religion."[20]

Machiavelli hates tyrants with all his soul; he spares no epithet in denouncing them, and devotes much energy to analyzing how to remove them. He has not lost his democratic faith. His call for a brief period of iron rule is a choice of the lesser of two evils: if the corruption continued, a real tyranny would be just a matter of time (making it even harder to restore free institutions), whereas freedom can be preserved if a good man can be found to put the state back in order. Just as it is sometimes necessary temporarily to resort to evil actions to achieve worthy objectives, so a period of dictatorship is sometimes the only hope for freedom. If, in a corrupt state, liberty "has to be introduced or maintained, then it will be necessary to reduce the state to a monarchical, rather than a republican, form of government; for men whose turbulence could not be controlled by the simple force of law can be controlled . . . only an almost regal power."[21]

The paradox is not as great as might appear at first blush. We need only consider Machiavelli's favorite hero, Moses, to understand what he has in mind. Moses exercised dictatorial power, but that awesome power was used to create freedom. Had the Israelites been capable of embracing freedom and virtue, either at Mount Sinai or on the edge of the Promised Land, Moses would not have resorted to extraordinary measures. But they weren't, and Moses was forced to lead.

We should not be outraged by Machiavelli's call for a temporary dictatorship as an effective means to either revivify or restore freedom. We have seen it done; indeed, we have done it ourselves, and it has been a great success, as when we set General Douglas MacArthur to serve as temporary dictator of Japan after the Second World War. MacArthur purged the warlords and imposed a democratic constitution, the success of which is plain for all to see. We did the same in Germany.

Was Nuremberg not a classic case of "extraordinary measures"? We "denazified" the country, hung many of the major leaders of the Third Reich, and forced all adults to answer detailed questionnaires about their activities and associations during Hitler's rule. We barred from positions of power and civic influence those who had actively participated in the Nazi regime. Then, as in Japan, we imposed a democratic constitution and kept an army in place to make sure it was respected. In Italy, the third partner of the wartime Axis, we drove the Nazi armies out of the country and then supported the post-fascist government as it conducted a purge similar to that in Germany and Japan.

The bloody story of the rise and defeat of fascism could have been lifted right out of Machiavelli's notebooks. Italy and Germany were highly civilized nations and had created lively democratic political systems. Yet over time, they turned away from civic virtues and became totalitarian tyrannies. Just as Machiavelli predicted, the tyrants came to power only after the people had become corrupt, as proven by the fact that fascism was a mass movement; Hitler and Mussolini came to power on the crest of a great wave of genuine popularity. Each had become the most popular political figure in his country, and the Fascist and Nazi parties attracted more support than any others. The regimes of Hitler and Mussolini remained enormously popular, and the opposition in Italy and Germany never attracted enough domestic political support to seriously threaten the regime. In both cases, opposition came only from small elites. Mussolini was removed by a coup organized by top officials of the regime, and then only when it was clear that the war was hopelessly lost. There was a similar plot to assassinate Hitler, but the conspirators' luck failed. Yet, just as Machiavelli knew it would, the spirit of freedom lived on in the people, and it was possible for the victorious Allies to restore democracy. But the restoration of democracy had to come from outside the corrupt system; the Germans, Italians, and Japanese could not have accomplished it themselves, any more than the peoples of the Soviet Empire could have won their own freedom without the Western victory in the Cold War.

Nuremberg was just what Machiavelli has in mind when he talks about the use of an almost regal power to save a corrupt republic: relentless prosecution of the old regime, followed by dramatic public executions of the leading criminals, thereby producing catharsis for the people and awe of the avenger who has temporarily come to set things right. Something of the sort should have been imposed on the fallen tyrannies of the Soviet Empire. Failure to call the Communist tyrants to account permitted the old elites to recycle themselves as new businessmen and politicians, thereby discrediting both business and politics. The behavior of the West at the end of the Cold War violated the Machiavellian injunction to remain true to your own rules. Instead of insisting that the Communist tyrants be called to account, Western leaders from George Bush to Helmut Kohl and François Mitterrand never raised the issue, and with very rare exceptions the Soviet Bloc dictators were never charged with criminal activity. This was an enormous setback to the cause of freedom and gravely weakened the authority of the fledgling governments. Remember Machiavelli's lesson that fear rests on "dread of punishment." The new democrats, having failed to punish the tyrants, were insufficiently feared by the people, and thus could not rule effectively.

The failure to purge the Communist tyrants violated another of Machiavelli's rules for the salvation of corrupt enterprises: you must defend the principles on which your society rests. In a chapter in the *Discourses* entitled "It Is a Bad Example to Ignore a Law, Especially by Its Author . . ." Machiavelli tells of the time when Savonarola, despite great opposition in Florence, managed to pass a law providing for condemned persons to appeal their sentences. Shortly thereafter, however, Savonarola denied this right to five men sentenced to death for plotting to bring the Medici back to power, prompting Machiavelli to write, "This ruined his reputation more than any other act."[22] In like manner, Machiavelli would judge harshly men like George Bush and James Baker for failing to enforce the virtuous standards of free societies against their tyrannical enemies. He would chastize the IMF and its supporters for failing to enforce the virtuous standards of the market, and he would denounce Bill Clinton for both of these sins, and for violating the very strictures against sexual harassment that he authored himself.

Businessmen know that corrupt corporations are best returned to health by dictatorial methods. Our laws enable such companies to be placed in "receivership" to navigate the crisis. The same was done to the District of Columbia in the late 1990s, after the nation's capital was thoroughly corrupted during the tenure of Mayor Marion Barry, and to New York City in the seventies.

The problem is to find a suitable leader, a good man willing to enter into evil to accomplish good ends. Such men are in short supply; good men shy from evil, and evil men are not interested in good ends.

It will . . . be exceedingly rare that a good man should be found willing to employ wicked means to become prince, even though his final object be good; or that a bad man, after having become prince, should be willing to labor for good, and that it should appeal to him to use well that which he has acquired through evil.[23]

That is why Machiavelli wrote *The Prince,* which is simultaneously a recruiting document for a new prince and a handbook for his rule. He is not optimistic that he will find the right man, knowing full well that leaders like Moses are rare. Without such a new prince, the downfall of a corrupt regime usually leads only to more corruption, a further erosion of freedom, and a greater likelihood of a durable tyranny. Nearly five centuries later, Machiavelli's country provided a clear example of this problem.

From the end of the Second World War to the end of the Cold War, the Italian political system was blocked because the major opposition party, the Communists, threatened both Italian democracy and the stability of the Western Alliance. Political leaders spent decades in power, the archetypal figure being Giulio Andreotti, whose career began with his position as aide to the first postwar prime minister and ended shortly after the fall of the Berlin Wall. Doomed to remain in power or opposition, all parties sank into corruption, producing an elaborate system of payoffs and kickbacks that enriched businesses and parties according to their political weight. The last political party to become a major player in this system was the Socialist party, and the man who accomplished it by leading the Socialists to national power was Bettino Craxi. Having arrived late at the public trough, the Socialists were in a hurry to catch up with their peers, and the quantity of bribes and kickbacks seems to have mounted during Craxi's years as prime minister in the early 1980s, and continued afterward as he and Andreotti cooperated in the division of the spoils.

In many ways Craxi was an outstanding leader. He was one of a handful of courageous politicians who led the parliamentary struggle that led to the installation of American cruise and Pershing missiles on Italian soil, thereby depriving the Soviet Union of the opportunity to blackmail Western Europe with a new generation of medium-range missiles. And Craxi was a mortal threat to the Communists, whom he ceaselessly challenged in every forum. Without him, communism might not have been defeated, and the revival of Italy as a major political force could not have been accomplished.

Moreover, Craxi was an exceptional politician. He organized a successful coup to take over the Socialist party in the late seventies and within a few years had become prime minister, even though his party never received even 15 percent of the popular vote. These remarkable accomplishments entitled him to write an introduction to an edition of *The Prince* at the height of his power. He fell to his ruin amidst the great scandals of the early nineties, when the vast network of corruption was exposed by the politically active judges who later crushed Berlusconi. I do not know whether Craxi and his associates were more corrupt than their predecessors, but they created an image of high living that significantly distinguished them from all other Italian political organizations. During the Craxi years, the Socialists were invariably at the center of the most luxurious festivities, and Socialist ministers surrounded themselves with the most glamorous women. The Christian Democrats who came before them were largely colorless figures, and although they were the creators of the corrupt system, they did not flaunt their wealth. The Communists were equally corrupt, but their great internal discipline kept secret the amount of their wealth and the sources of their payoffs, which included direct cash subsidies from the Soviet Union and commissions on virtually all commercial transactions between Italy and the U.S.S.R. They were so certain of the reliability of their own people that they repeatedly described themselves as the "party with clean hands."

Not so the Socialists, and they paid a terrible price for their revelry and for their failure to realize that even the Italian system can change. Once the great purge began, Craxi was widely demonized as the high priest of corruption. His trial in Milan was broadcast live on national television, and the country ground to a standstill as people stopped to watch the dramatic confrontation between the former prime minister and an aggressive young prosecutor. Angry crowds gathered outside his hotel in Rome and pelted him with coins as he came and went. Condemned and sentenced to multiple prison terms, he fled the country to a comfortable villa in Hamamet, Tunisia. Now in disgraced exile and worsening health, Craxi's precipitous fall from the heights of power exemplifies Machiavelli's warnings that corruption can destroy even the most successful leaders, and that those who fall from power will receive nothing but ingratitude from those they led.

But no new prince came forward to set things in proper order. Berlusconi's failure has already been described, and the men of the center-left who succeeded him have concentrated their energies on solidifying their own power, not on breaking the link between government and business that lies at the heart of national corruption. On the contrary; the post-Berlusconi government rather excelled at placing political allies at the top of corporations, and most of the privatizations, which might have weakened the role of the state, have merely transferred shares from the treasury to reliable bankers and industrialists. Control remains in the hands of the political parties, and any threat to their hegemony is quickly dealt with by the judges, who have still not prosecuted any of the left-wing leaders who were part of the corruption. Inevitably, payoffs and kickbacks have resumed.

It might have been possible for Italy to rid itself of the majority of the corrupt leaders, but it would have required a monumental effort to destroy not only all the old political parties but also the state's vast control over major industries. This task could only have been accomplished by an exceptional leader, or from some outside force. Neither has appeared.

In Japan and Germany after the war, and in Washington, D.C., and New York City on the verge of bankruptcy, new

princes from the outside representing uncorrupted powers imposed reforms on broken enterprises. That is a lot easier than finding a tough leader of exceptional resolve and exemplary moral qualities within the corrupt system, one willing to do the evil things that alone can save freedom.

Yet it can be done. Abraham Lincoln, who showed few signs of greatness before the awful crisis of the Union, found within himself both moral courage and a willingness to enter into evil—waging one of the bloodiest wars in history to advance freedom in America. And when the Ottoman Empire was finally shattered in the First World War, a military officer, Kemal Ataturk, used the army to defend Turkey, rout her enemies, and then completely transform his country, and put it on the road to freedom. As Machiavelli wisely forecast, both Lincoln and Ataturk were reluctant to undertake their great missions. Lincoln sought to preserve the Union by all means, and went to war as a last resort. Ataturk sought to preserve Ottoman rule, and only abolished it when the alternatives became impossible. By the end, Lincoln had won the war, preserved the Union, and abolished slavery; Ataturk had won the war, abolished Ottoman rule, and created a secular Turkish state, one that renounced her historic claim to be the legitimate guide of the Islamic world. In time, Turkey became a parliamentary republic.

The force of Ataturk's virtue outlasted his own life, evi-

dence of the Machiavellian principle that temporary dictatorial rule can be used to rescue the republic from corruption and crisis. As we saw earlier, when Turkey was overwhelmed in the late 1970s by the greatest wave of mass terrorism ever recorded, the army seized power, eliminated terrorism, restructured the republic, and returned to the barracks, leaving the country in the able hands of Turgut Ozal. Nearly twenty years later, in 1997, the army again intervened, this time without directly exercising power, to bring down a governmental coalition composed of a corrupt secular party and Islamic forces seeking to impose religious institutions on Ataturk's republic.

These were exceptional men. Most of the time, enterprises in such dire straits are not rescued; they go down to ruin, either destroyed or enslaved. Even such great leaders as Lincoln and Ataturk were able to prevail only after great bloodshed and misery. Wise leaders, the virtuous men and women Machiavelli seeks to educate, fight hard to prevent terrible crises. That way, the drastic remedies contained in *The Prince* will not be necessary.

CONCLUSION

Even after a half a millennium, Machiavelli's advice to leaders is as contemporary as tomorrow. He goes to the essence every time. He doesn't allow us the comfort of easy generalizations or soothing moralisms. He wants leaders to play for the highest stakes of all—the advancement of the human enterprise and the defense of the common good—and it infuriates him to see leaders of corporations, religions, armies, and nations ignoring the basic rules of power.

Machiavelli became infamous because of his advice to would-be leaders coping with mortal crisis, but most of his rules of power are for leaders in ordinary circumstances. He believes that if those rules are vigorously applied, the crises will be less likely, and drastic measures won't be necessary. Not that leadership is ever for the fainthearted; anyone in a position of power will be under constant attack from people ea-

ger to dominate him. Those who wield power must be prepared to fight at all times.

Machiavelli's rules rest upon a clear-eyed view of human
nature. If you think that people are basically good and, left to
their own devices, will create loving communities and good
governments, you've learned nothing from him. Machiavelli's
world is populated by people more inclined to do evil than
good, whose instincts are distinctly antisocial. These are your
followers and bosses, colleagues and employees, and, above
all, your competitors and enemies. The only way to dominate
your foes and get your friends and allies to work together is to
use power effectively.

Leaders must fight their way to the top, and then guard
against the corruption that inevitably sets in as soon as they
succeed. This second battle is the toughest, for it is not waged
against obvious enemies, but against friends, colleagues, fellow citizens and trusted advisers—and even against one's own
selfish impulses. These rules are particularly urgent for us,
since we are quite clearly in danger of falling into corruption.
The 1996 American presidential elections pitted Bill Clinton—whose image is called to mind by Machiavelli's pages
describing "effeminate states and indolent leaders"—against
Bob Dole, the man who felt that virtue was an unsuitable
theme for political debate. Machiavelli teaches us that virtue
is far and away the most important issue. A nation that will not

discuss virtue and hold its leaders accountable for their corruption is in desperate need of renewal.

Machiavelli asks, "Have the people become corrupt? If they have not, traditional means of national renewal should work, provided virtuous leadership is found in time. America has utilized several means of renewal in its history, from periodic religious revivals (and there is considerable evidence that one is currently underway) to Watergatelike punishments of the mighty when they transgress our standards. The West has an abundance of people capable of good leadership, but most of our actual leaders, like their counterparts in the rest of the world, have fallen far short of Machiavelli's standards. The last member of the heroic generation of the 1970s and 1980s, Pope John Paul II, is near the end of his religious and political mission, and it is hard to see any new leader of his stature or the stature of Ronald Reagan, Margaret Thatcher, King Juan Carlos, Lech Walesa, Lee Kwan Yu, Deng Xiaoping, Nelson Mandela, and Vaclav Havel, who transformed the world. If new and more virtuous leaders do not emerge, it is only a matter of time before we are either dominated by our enemies or sink into a more profound crisis.

Machiavelli warns us in a clarion voice that if corruption has reached down into the public so that the people are no longer outraged by the moral and political corruption of their leaders; if, instead of demanding laws and leaders that defend virtue and advance the common good, the people emulate the self-indulgence and indolence of the leaders, then, even if our enemies or Fortune spare us, we are on the road to tyranny. Some fear that the seeming indifference of the American public to the revelations about the moral and political corruption of the Clinton administration and the president himself is evidence that the corruption has spread far and wide. There is similar evidence in the sports world, where some governing authorities have contented themselves with token punishments of star athletes and of corrupt officials of the International Olympic Committee instead of the quick and terrible blows Machiavelli advocates. If that is the case, we will soon find ourselves in the same desperate crisis that drove Machiavelli to call for a new dictator to set things aright.

In either case, we need Machiavellian wisdom and leadership. Without it, our fine political, religious, economic, and athletic institutions will go to ruin, as have so many in other times and places. Machiavelli wrote in the hope of inspiring brave and talented men and women to leave the comforts of ease and luxury and enter the lists to fight for freedom and virtue. He failed. No new prince came forward to rescue Italy from its decadence, and even today Machiavelli's words of scorn and despair are a deadly accurate description of his country.

We must do better.

NOTES

INTRODUCTION

1. James Atkinson and David Sices, eds., *Machiavelli and His Friends: Their Personal Correspondence* (De Kalb, Ill., 1996), p. 264.
2. Sebastian de Grazia, *Machiavelli in Hell* (New York, 1994), p. 21.

CHAPTER ONE: "THE COURSE OF HUMAN EVENTS"

1. *Discourses,* I, 46.*
2. *Discourses,* I, 37.
3. *Discourses,* II, 9.
4. *Discourses,* I, 1.
5. Ralph Waldo Emerson, "Self-Reliance," in *Essays* (Boston, 1841).
6. Machiavelli, "Ingratitudine," trans. Sebastian de Grazia, in de Grazia, *Machiavelli in Hell* (New York, 1994), p. 83.

---

*Source used throughout: Niccolò Machiavelli, *Discorsi Sopra la Prima Deca di Tito Livio* (Torino, 1983). (Corrado Vivanti, editor)

7. Donald Kagan, *On the Origins of War and the Preservation of Peace* (New York, 1995), p. 570.
8. Ibid.
9. Franz-Olivier Giesbert, *Le Président* (Paris, 1990), p. 384.
10. See Zheng Yi, *Scarlet Memorial: Tales of Cannibalism in Modern China* (New York, 1996).
11. Alexander Zinoviev, *Le Héros de notre jeunesse* (Paris, 1984), p. 42.
12. Keegan, *Wall Street Journal,* March 27, 1997.
13. George P. Shultz, *Turmoil and Triumph: My Years As Secretary of State* (New York, 1993), p. 649.
14. My thanks to Ms. Natalie Hayes for the neat turn of phrase.
15. *Discourses,* III, 10.

CHAPTER TWO: "LUCK"

1. Victor Niederhoffer, *The Education of a Speculator* (New York, 1997), pp. 5–6.
2. Winston Churchill, *My Early Life: A Roving Commission* (New York, 1930), p. 276.
3. Bryan Burrough and John Helyar, *Barbarians at the Gate* (New York, 1991), p. 17.
4. *Discourses,* II, 29.
5. Burke Davis, *The Civil War: Strange and Fascinating Facts* (New York, 1982), p. 20.
6. Ibid., p. 21.
7. *Discourses,* III, 63.
8. *Discourses,* III, 1.
9. Ichak Adizes, *The Pursuit of Prime* (Santa Monica and Boston, 1996), p. 236.

CHAPTER THREE: "THE WAR OF POLITICS"

1. Isaiah Berlin, "The Originality of Machiavelli," in *Against the Current: Essays in the History of Ideas* (London, 1955), p. 40.

2. Robert Penn Warren, *All the King's Men* (New York, n.d.), p. 257.
3. Anton La Guardia, "General's crush on Lollobrigida saved troops from attack," *The Telegraph* (London), 2 January 1998.
4. Letter to Francesco Vettori, 3 August 1514.
5. *The Florentine Histories*, V, 1.
6. *The Prince*, 14.
7. John Keegan, *Wall Street Journal*, 27 March 1997.
8. Letter from General von Moltke to Dr. J. K. Bluntschli, 11 December 1880.
9. *Discourses*, I, 6.
10. Sebastian de Grazia, *Machiavelli in Hell* (New York, 1994), p. 135.
11. Machiavelli, *Clizia*, Act 3, trans. Sebastian de Grazia, cited in de Grazia, op. cit., p. 137.
12. *The Art of War*, 7.
13. Paul Flick, *The Dysfunctional President* (New York, 1995).
14. Thomas E. Ricks, *Making the Corps* (New York, 1997), p. 55.
15. *Discourses*, III, 10.
16. David Sapsted, "Employers Stop Trying to Blunt Cupid's Arrow," *The Telegraph* (London), 5 February 1998.
17. *The Art of War*, 7.

CHAPTER FOUR: "OF GOOD AND EVIL"
1. *The Prince*, VI.
2. *The Discourses*, I, 3.
3. *Exodus* 32:26–28.
4. *Discourses*, III, 30.
5. Machiavelli, *Clizia*, Act 4, Trans. Sebastian de Grazia, cited in de Grazia, *Machiavelli in Hell* (New York, 1984), p. 301

6. From Steven F. Hayward, *Churchill on Leadership* (New York, 1997), p. 153.
7. Lieut.-Gen. Sir Garnet J. Wolseley, *The Soldier's Pocket Book* (London, 1882), p. 162.
8. *The Prince,* 17.
9. *Discourses,* I, 10.
10. *Discourses,* I, 26.
11. *The Prince,* 6.
12. *Discourses,* III, 28.
13. Richard Pipes, *Three "Whys" of the Russian Revolution* (New York, 1997), p. 40.
14. *Discourses,* I, 58.
15. *Discourses,* II, 2.
16. *Discourses,* I, 58.
17. *Discourses,* I, 2.
18. *Discourses,* I, 58.
19. *Discourses,* I, 12.

CHAPTER FIVE: "HOW TO RULE"

1. *Discourses,* I, 3.
2. George S. Patton, Jr., *War As I Knew It* (Boston, 1947), p. 336.
3. Walter Laqueur, *Terrorism* (New York, 1978), p. 146.
4. *The Art of War,* 7.
5. *Discourses,* III, 1.
6. "Discursus florentinarum rerum post mortem junioris Laurentii Medices."
7. *Discourses,* III, 51.
8. *Discourses,* II, 2.
9. B. H. Liddell Hart, *Great Captains Unveiled* (London, 1989), p. 110.
10. *The Prince,* 15.
11. *Discourses,* III, 22.
12. Douglas Southall Freeman, *George Washington* (New York, 1952), p. 435.

13. *The Prince,* 17.
14. *Gazette of the United States* (Philadelphia), 19 November 1794.
15. *The Prince,* 19.
16. E. V. Walter, *Terror and Resistance* (New York, Oxford, 1969), p. 176.
17. *Discourses,* III, 3 and 30.
18. Machiavelli, *Discorsi,* ed. Corrado Vivanti (Milan, 1983), 367 n.
19. Joseph Farah and Sarah Foster, "WorldNet Daily," 24 June 1997.
20. *Panorama,* 12 June 1997.
21. *Discourses,* I, 18.

CHAPTER SIX: "FREEDOM"

1. *Discourses,* I, 16.
2. William Drozdiak, "First Lady Takes Up Cause of East European Women," *Washington Post,* 7 December 1997.
3. *The Prince,* 5.
4. Perry Flint, "The Buck Stops Lower," *ASAP,* September 1995.
5. *Discourses,* III, 8.
6. *Discourses,* I, 18.
7. *Discourses,* I, 24.
8. Paul Craig Roberts, "Corruption Is a Cancer That Grows," *Conservative Current,* 12 August 1997.
9. *Discourses,* III, 1.
10. *Discourses,* III, 1.
11. Ibid.
12. Bernard Lewis, "Ottoman Observers of Ottoman Decline," in Bernard Lewis, ed., *Islam in History* (Chicago and La Salle, 1993), p. 212.
13. Harry Dunphy (Associated Press), "IMF, World Bank Link Aid to 'Good Governance,'" *Washington Times,* 21 August 1997.

14. John Train, *Famous Financial Fiascos* (Burlington, Vt., 1995), p. 12.
15. Allan H. Meltzer, *Moral Hazard Goes Global: The IMF, Mexico, and Asia* (Washington, D.C., January 1998).
16. Lawerence B. Lindsey, *The Benefits of Bankruptcy* (Washington, D.C., January 1998), p. 3.
17. *Discourses,* I, 58.
18. Alexis de Tocqueville, *Democracy in America* (New York, 1972), p. 226–27.
19. *Discourses,* I, 17.
20. *The Prince,* 18.
21. *Discourses,* I, 18.
22. *Discourses,* I, 45.
23. Ibid.

ACKNOWLEDGMENTS

This book grew out of conversations with interns and colleagues at the American Enterprise Institute, after I discovered that study of Machiavelli was waning, even at major universities. I am indebted to Chris DeMuth, Nic Eberstadt, Irving Kristol, Allan Meltzer, Charles Murray, and David Wurmser of AEI and to Jimmy Cayne, Gertrude Himmelfarb, and Tom O'Connell, all of whom found errors and made helpful suggestions.

This book rests on the shoulders of Sebastian de Grazia, whose wonderful biography, *Machiavelli in Hell,* is an inspiration. I was lucky to have the benefit of his encouragement and advice, on both Machiavelli and Tuscan wines.

I was fortunate to have exceptional research assistance from Adam Storch, Shannon Mangiameli, Joachim Sorensen, and Marieke Widmann.

Special thanks to my editor and publisher, Truman Talley at St. Martin's Press, who fully deserves his reputation as one of America's best, and to my agents Lynn Chu and Glen Hartley.

As in the past, the Freedom Chair at AEI has been supported by a group of philanthropic entrepreneurs. I hope this little book provides them with a measure of the satisfaction they deserve. Thanks also to Michael Milken.

No book turns out exactly the way the author expected, and I was surprised that this one has so much to do with religion, and particularly with Moses. My understanding of Moses comes largely from Rabbi Augusto Segre, a hero of the Italian Resistance, a rare Jewish lecturer within the Vatican, the author of a profound biography of Moses, and the man who married Barbara and me in Rome twenty-five years ago, a great blessing indeed. Our third child was born the day Augusto died and is named after him. *Machiavelli on Modern Leadership* is gratefully dedicated to his memory.

INDEX

INDEX

INDEX

INDEX

INDEX